# COMPUTERS
## OUR LIFELINE

**3**

Based on NEP

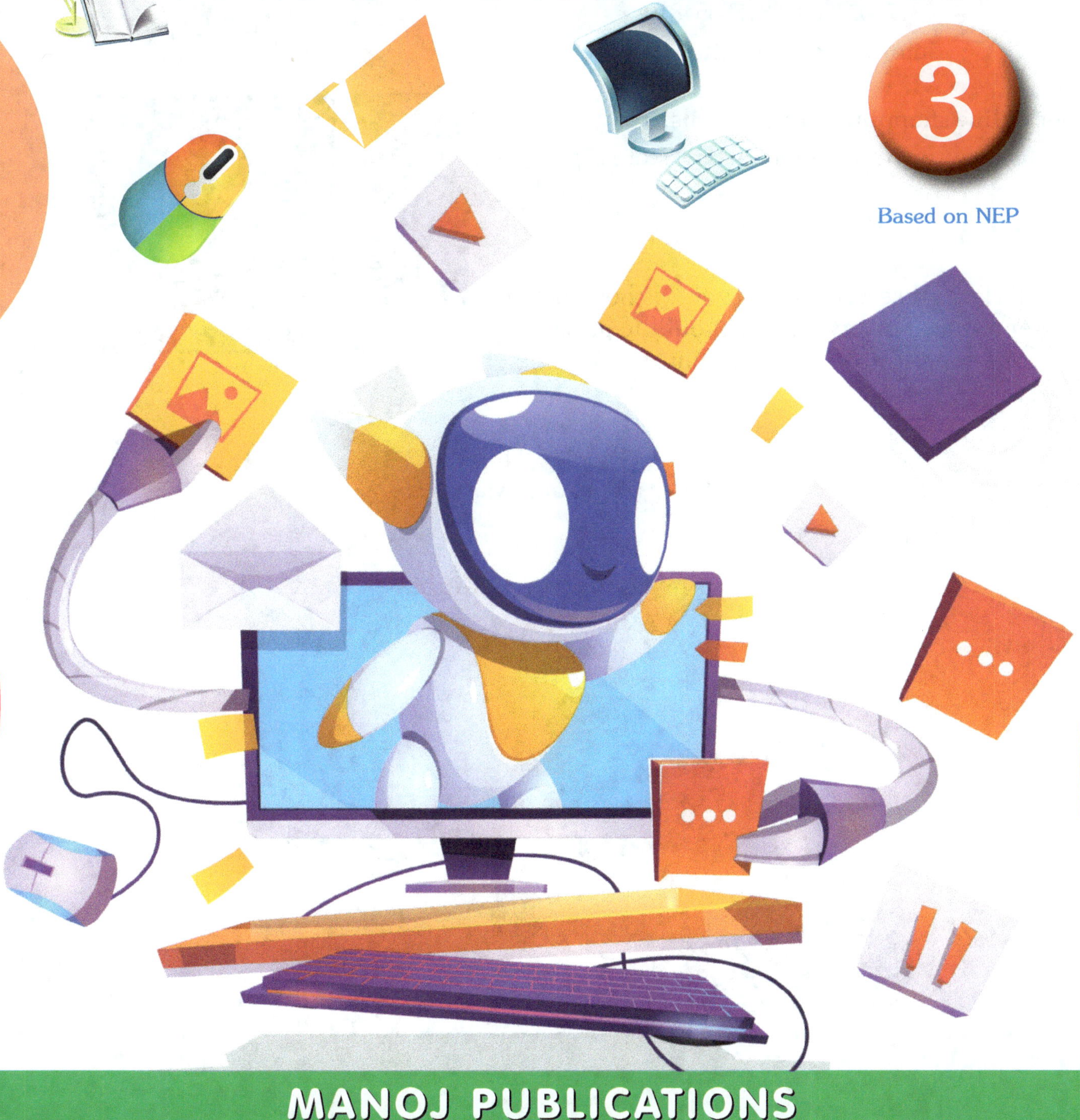

## MANOJ PUBLICATIONS

# COMPUTERS
## Our Lifeline - 3

Publishers:

**MANOJ PUBLICATIONS**

761, Main Road, Burari, Delhi-110084 (INDIA)

Mobile : 09999476076, 09868112194,
08178823569, 08178854810

Email : info@manojpublications.com

**For online shopping visit our website :**

Website : www.sawanonlinebookstore.com

ISBN : 978-81-310-1641-1

*Concept:*

**Puneet Gupta**
M.B.A. (William & Mary, U.S.A.)

*Edited by:*

**Davinder Singh Minhas**
**Rohan Kumar**

# PREFACE

This is the Age of Computers. In every nook and corner of the globe, computers have made their presence felt, be it school, office, post office, bank, shop, mall, hotel, restaurant, airport, railway station, Metro station and so on. Needless to say, they have become our lifeline as we can't do anything without them. In order to keep pace with the modern world, it is important to familiarise our children with computer applications right from the start. They ought to be taught the uses of computer in a lucid, interesting and enjoyable style: from basic to intermediate to advanced level.

Keeping in view the requirements of students, all the books in the series— **Computers : Our Lifeline**—have been designed to meet the purpose of acquiring a sound in-depth knowledge on computers with their uses. The contents of the books are based entirely on recently approved NEP (National Educational Policy).

The chapters in all the books contain a fairly good amount of illustrations which make the text very easy to understand. There are many computer books flooding the market. Our books are the books with a difference in order that they are well equipped with exhaustive exercises which test a student's mental horizon by making him take Formative Assessment as well as Summative Assessment. The knowledge of the latest software with their applications and types of computer language have been made available. Nay, students have been introduced to coding, the process of designing computer apps. The main goal of books in the series is to make a student computerate, *i.e.* computer literate.

We sincerely hope that all the books in this series will prove fruitful both to students and teachers. We shall be highly pleased to receive constructive suggestions in order to make the series more qualitative in the forthcoming editions.

– Author

# CONTENTS

# 1   The Computer System

## COMPUTER SYSTEM

As you all know, a computer is a very useful electronic machine that gets instructions from you and works accordingly.

So, you can define the computer as follows: A computer is an electronic device. It accepts data and instructions as input and after processing, it gives information as output.

A computer runs on electricity. It has made our life very comfortable.

**A labelled diagram of a computer system is shown below :**

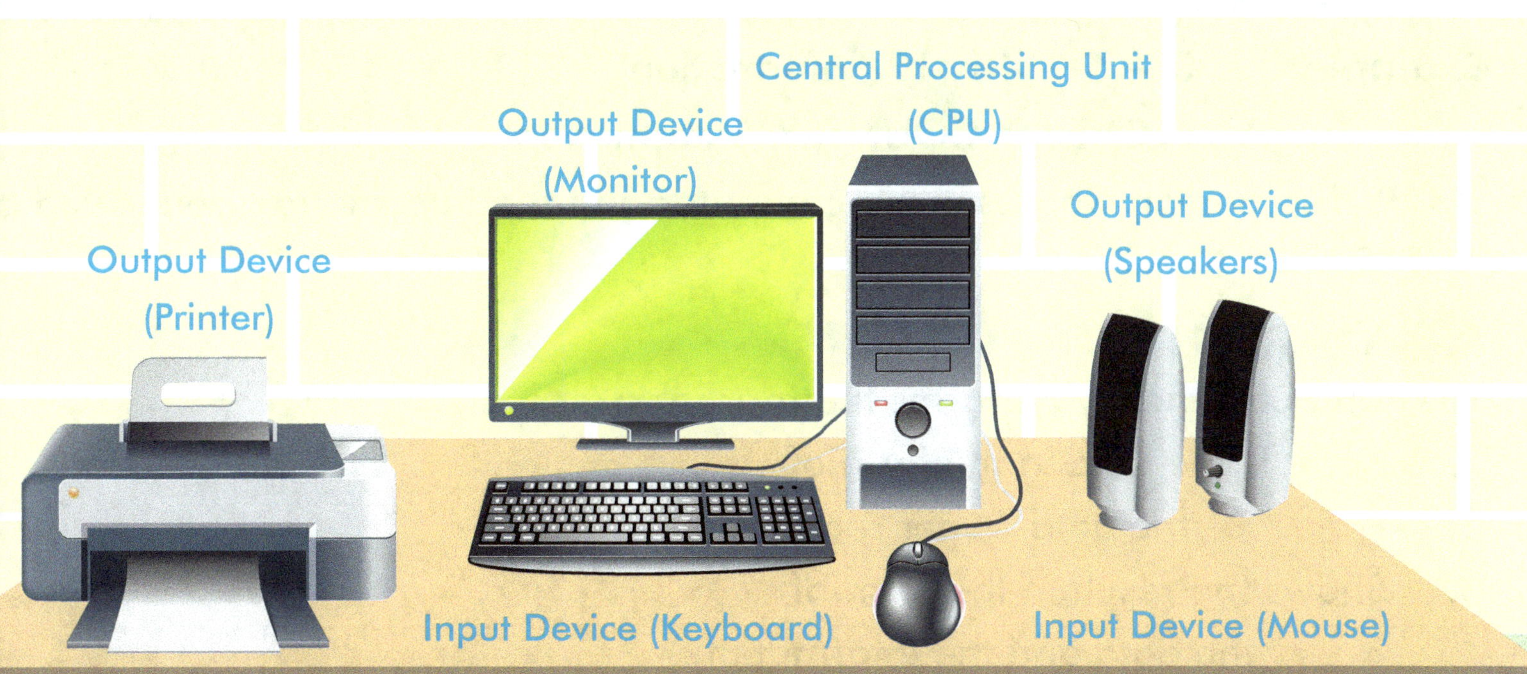

# Data and Information

A computer is an electronic device which receives data from the user, processes it and converts it into information.

Before moving ahead let's know about some terms like data, process, information and user.

**DATA**: Data can also be called as raw information, which can include words, numbers, images and sounds. It is processed in order to produce information which is meaningful to the user.

Data is a collection of facts that has no meaning for the user until it becomes information.

**Example**:  +, 3, 5, 4, +, = (data)

COUNTRY, MY, I, LOVE (data)

**PROCESS**: The processor of the computer takes data and processes it to convert it into meaningful information.

+, 3, 5, 4, +, =          3 + 5 + 4 =          12

**Data** → **Process** → **Information**

**INFORMATION**: The result of data that we get after processing is called information. It is meaningful and organized. This is helpful to the user in making decisions.

**Example**:  3 + 5 + 4 = 12 (information)

I LOVE MY COUNTRY. (information)

**USER**: The person who uses the computer and the information generated by it, is called a user.

## WORKING OF COMPUTER

The computer mainly performs the four jobs:

1.  Accepts the data in the form of input.
2.  Processes the data as per requirement.
3.  Shows the result in the form of output.
4.  Stores the data and the information.

The above working can be shown in the form of a block diagram.

**Block Diagram**

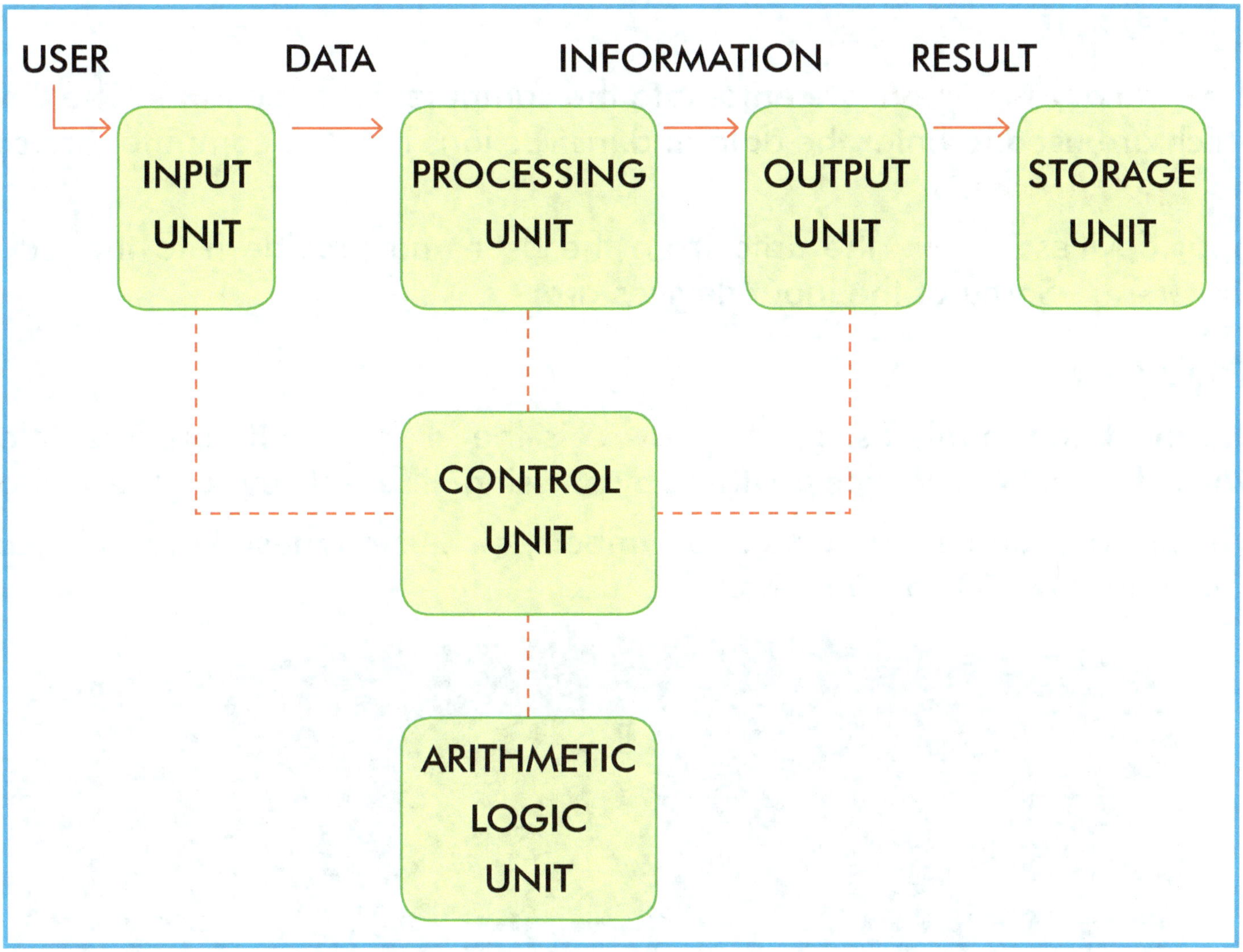

The **block diagram** shows:

1. The **data** given by the **user** is entered as **input** through different **input devices** like keyboard, mouse, scanner, etc.

2. The **input devices** further send the data for **processing** to the Central Processing Unit (CPU).

3. After getting **processed**, the data gets changed into **information** and the result is shown in the form of **output** through different **output devices**, like monitor, printer, etc.

*Working of the computer on the basis of Input, Processing and Output cycle is called IPO cycle.*

4. Now, the user can **store** the information for the future use by using the **storage devices**.

This is how a computer works. Let us now study about Input, Process, Output and Storage units.

## INPUT

The data or instructions we enter into the computer is called Input. The devices which are used to enter the data and instructions into the computer are called the input devices.

Input devices receive the data from the user and provide it to the CPU for processing. Some of the input devices are:

## Keyboard

The most commonly used input device is the keyboard. It contains different types of keys. We can type anything by pressing different keys on the keyboard.

We can type letters, numbers and symbols, etc., using these keys. A keyboard has generally 101 to 105 keys.

Keyboard

## Mouse

Mouse is an input device used to draw and select objects on the computer screen. It is also called a pointing device.

A mouse consists of two buttons and a scroll wheel. The bottom of the mouse is flat and contains a mechanism that detects the movement of the mouse.

Whenever we move the mouse in any direction, an arrow on the screen moves in the same direction. This arrow is called mouse pointer.

Mouse

Mouse Pointer

## Mouse Substitutes

There are many other devices that perform the same function as the mouse but in different ways.

Touch screen

**Touch screen**: It helps us enter input by simply touching the screen. Here the input is recorded when a finger comes in contact with the screen. This finger acts as the pointing device. We use touch screens generally in the ATMs (Automated Teller Machines) of banks.

Track ball

**Track ball**: It is a pointing device that looks like an upside-down mouse. Here, the ball that controls the movement of the cursor is placed on top. It also has two buttons and serves the same function as the mouse. To move the pointer, one rotates the ball with one's thumb, fingers or the palm of the hand.

**Light pen**: A light pen is a pointing device that can be used to select anything on the computer screen by simply pointing to it or for drawing figures directly on the screen. Clicking is performed by pressing the pen on the screen.

Light pen

## Scanner

Scanner

A scanner is an input device. It is used to send images and text into the computer. It is just like a photocopy machine that copies the image or text and shows it on the computer. We can scan photographs, drawings, documents, logos, etc.

## Joystick

A joystick is an input device which has a vertical stick on it. You can move the stick in any direction in order to make the pointer on the screen move in the same way. We use it mainly to play computer games.

Joystick

Microphone

## Microphone

A microphone is an input device. It is used to record c
sound into a computer system.



## PROCESS

The computer processes data and changes it into information with the help o
a processor. For example, CPU (Central Processing Unit).

## CPU

CPU is the Central Processing Unit. It is also called
the brain of the computer. All types of processing are
done by the CPU. The CPU is also called Processor or
Microprocessor.

Central Processing Unit

The CPU receives input from input devices and processes
it before providing the processed result to the output
devices.

For instance, if you want to add any numbers like 40 and 30, type 40 and 30
and give the instruction to add them through an input device like keyboard
The computer will process this and give the result, *i.e.* 70.

The CPU has further two units and allots the work to the corresponding units

1.  **Arithmetic Logic Unit (ALU)**: It is the part which performs arithmetical
    comparative and logical operations. Arithmetical operations include
    addition, subtraction, multiplication and division.

    Comparative operations involve comparing one data to another. For
    example: greater than, equal to or less than.

    Logical operations use conditions along with logical operators such as
    AND, OR and NOT.

2.  **Control Unit (CU)**: Being the control unit, it controls all the functions o
    a computer. It also checks the results given by ALU.

    It also checks what to do and when to do.

# OUTPUT

The result you get after processing the data is known as output. The output is provided by the different output devices either in the form of hard copy or soft copy. These output devices are monitor, printer and speakers.

## Monitor

A monitor is an output device that displays the output on the screen. Its other name is Visual Display Unit (VDU).

A monitor resembles a TV-screen. Both text and graphics can be displayed on it. Whatever you type on the keyboard comes on the monitor. The text or video you see on the monitor is called soft copy. There are various sizes of a monitor such as 14", 15", 17", 22", 26", etc.

Monitor

Monitors come in two major types:

CRT (Cathode Ray Tube) and LCD (Liquid Crystal Display)

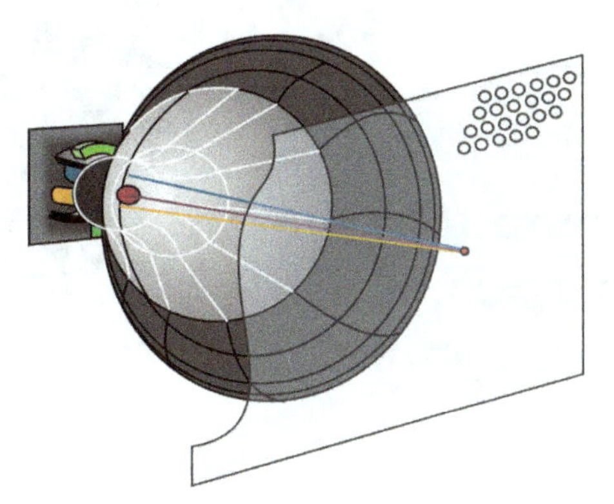

CRT monitor

LCD monitors

# Printer

A printer is an output device used to get the result on the paper called printouts. The result can be in the form of text and graphics. Printed information, which exists physically, is called hard copy.

There are different types of printers available like Dot Matrix, Laser, Inkjet Printer, etc.

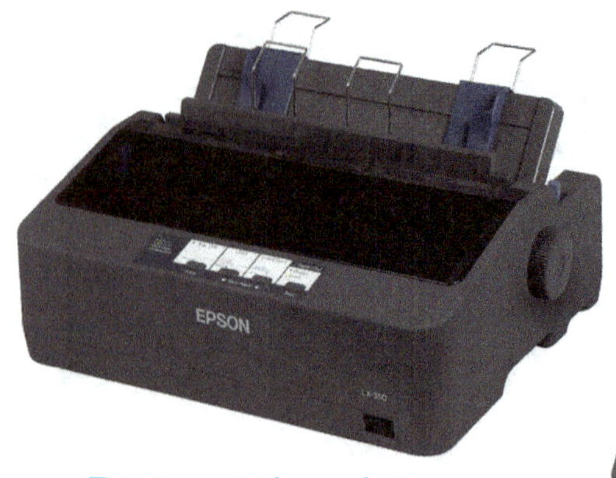

Dot matrix printer

Inkjet printer

Laser printer

# Speakers

Speakers are output devices that give output in the form of voice. Speakers typically come in a pair, which allow them to produce stereo sound. Through them you get the output in different sounds.

Speakers

 **STORAGE**

The data you enter or output you get, saved permanently into the computer, is called storage. The storage is done by different storage devices as follows:

# Hard Disk Drive

A hard disk is a storage device fixed inside the system unit. It is used in almost all computers. It has a large capacity and can store a large amount of data inside it.

Hard disk

Floppy disk    Floppy disk drive

# Floppy Disk Drive

The floppy disk drive is a storage device located in the front of the system unit. It helps you store or read data inside the floppy disk, also called a floppy.

## Do you know ?

*Floppy Disks are very sensitive to moisture and dust. They have a low data transfer rate. Hence, Many newer computers don't have a floppy drive.*

## CD and DVD Drives

The CD and DVD drives are storage devices located in the front of the system unit. They help read, store information in CDs and DVDs respectively.

CD/DVD    CD and DVD drive

Pen drive

## Pen Drive

The Pen drive is a very small and portable storage device that is most popularly used today. It is connected to the USB (Universal Serial Bus) port present on the system unit to read or write data.

## LET'S HAVE A LOOK

- A computer is an electronic machine that gets instructions from the user and works accordingly.
- A computer mainly performs the four jobs, *i.e.* Input, Process, Output and Storage.
- The data you enter into the computer is called Input.
- The processing is done by The Central Processing Unit (CPU).
- The result you get after processing is called Output.
- The input devices, like keyboard, mouse, scanner, etc., are used to input data.
- The output devices, like monitor, printer and speakers, show the output.
- The storage devices like hard disk drive, floppy disk drive, CD/DVD drive and pen drive, are used to store data permanently.

## BRAIN TEASER

**1.** **Write the answers to the following questions:**

a. Define a computer.

b. What are the four main jobs performed by the computer?

c. What is input? Name some input devices.

d. What is output? Name some output devices.

e. What are storage devices used for?

f. What is the function of the CPU?

2. **Write the names of the following:**

a.   Name the device that gives you output in the form of sound.

b.   Name the different parts of the CPU.

c.   Name the input device used to play games.

d.   Name the popularly used portable storage device.

e.   Name the different types of printers.

f.   Name two types of monitors available.

g.   Name the device that looks like an upside-down mouse.

3. **Multiple Choice Questions**

**Tick (✓) the correct answer:**

a.   The part of the CPU that controls the functions of the computer
   i.   MU ☐        ii.   ALU ☐        iii.   CU ☐

b.   You can enter data into the computer through
   i.    Input devices ☐
   ii.   Output devices ☐
   iii.  Storage devices ☐

c.   The device which is used to give hard copy
   i.   Keyboard ☐        ii.   Printer ☐        iii.   Monitor ☐

d.    The device that shows the results

    i.    Input device    ☐

    ii.   Output device   ☐

    iii.  Storage device  ☐

e.    Hard disk is a/an

    i.    Storage device  ☐

    ii.   Output device   ☐

    iii.  Input device    ☐

f.    The computer processes the data to convert it into

    i.    Instructions    ☐

    ii.   Commands        ☐

    iii.  Information     ☐

## 4.  Unjumble the letters and fill in the blanks:

a.    A computer is an ________________ machine.

| E | E | C | T | R | O | C | I | L | N |
|---|---|---|---|---|---|---|---|---|---|

b.    We get result through different ________________.

| U | O | T | T | D | U | E | S | P | C | E | V | I |
|---|---|---|---|---|---|---|---|---|---|---|---|---|

c.    The ________________ is done by CPU.

| S | G | P | C | S | E | I | O | R | N |
|---|---|---|---|---|---|---|---|---|---|---|

d.    ________________ performs Arithmetical and Logical operations.

| U | L | A |
|---|---|---|

e.    The results are stored in ________________ unit.

| O | S | R | G | T | E | A |
|---|---|---|---|---|---|---|

f.    The monitor displays the output in the form of ________________.

| T | S | Y | O | O | F | C | P |
|---|---|---|---|---|---|---|---|

5. **Write 'T' for true and 'F' for false in the boxes:**

   a.   A computer is a manual machine.

   b.   Output is the result we get after processing.

   c.   Data is a collection of facts that has no meaning for the user.

   d.   The computer stores data in a storage device.

   e.   The result of a printer is called soft copy.

   f.   The CPU does all the processing.

6. **Match the following devices with their names:**

   a.   Touch screen

   b.   Speakers

   c.   Pen drive

   d.   Hard disk

   e.   Printer

7. **Complete the following diagram:**

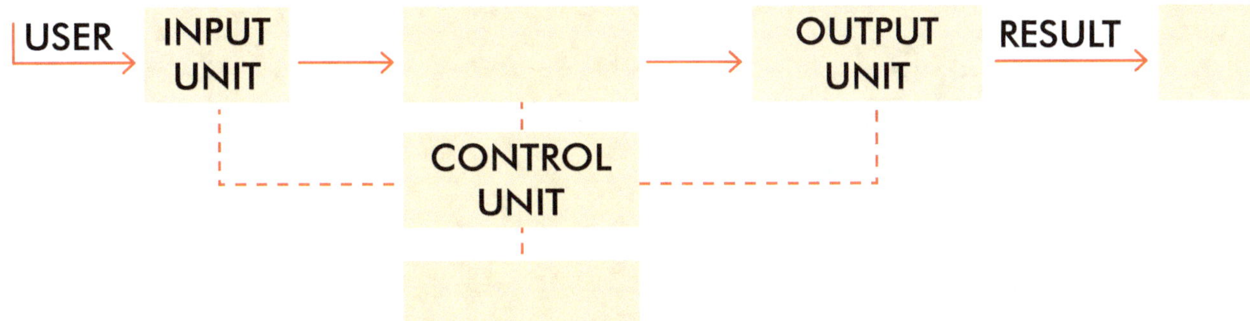

## FUN TIME

**Given below are some devices. Categorise them and write their names in their respective boxes.**

| Input Devices | Output Devices | Storage Devices | Processing Devices |
| --- | --- | --- | --- |
|  |  |  |  |

# Hardware and Software

## COMPONENTS OF COMPUTER SYSTEM

A computer is an electronic machine which consists of various parts. Some parts can be touched and seen like keyboard, mouse, monitor, etc. There are some parts which can be seen but cannot be touched like Windows, MS Word, Paint Brush, etc.

A computer works with the help of these parts which are known as its components. These components, when attached together in specific order, make up the term 'Computer System'.

These components are broadly classified into two parts: Hardware and Software.

## HARDWARE

Hardware defines the physical parts of the computer which can be touched and seen.

All these parts are attached to the computer with the help of wires called peripherals.

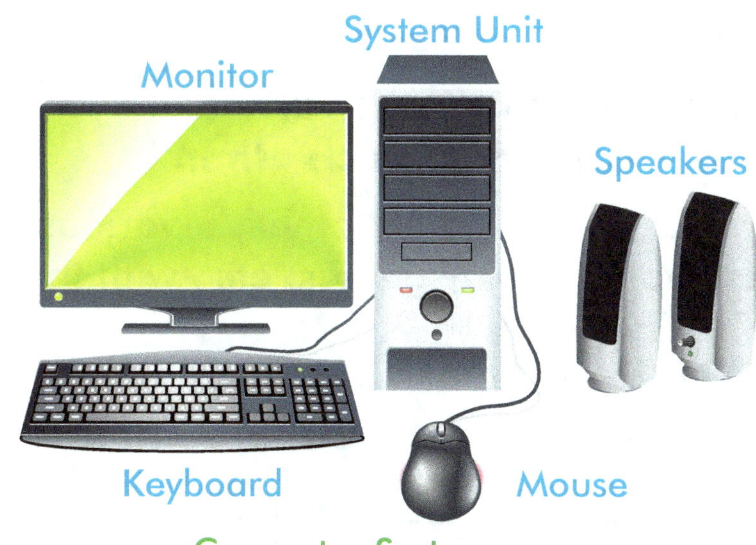

The main hardware parts of a computer system can be divided into four kinds of devices.

1. Input Devices

2. Output Devices

3. Processing Unit

4. Storage Devices

**You have already studied about the above-mentioned devices in the previous chapter. Here you will study about software.**

## SOFTWARE

Software refers to the hidden parts of a computer which cannot be touched. Software is a set of instructions, stored on disk drives or CD/DVDs, that tells the computer hardware what to do and how to perform a particular job.

Both Hardware and Software are the important parts of the computer. In the absence of any of these parts, the computer cannot function. In other words, without hardware, software is nothing and without software, hardware is a dumb machine.

**For example**, if we have a mouse (hardware) but do not have Paint program (software) in our computer, we cannot draw in the computer. Similarly, if we have Paint program (software) but do not have a mouse (hardware) attached to it, we cannot draw either. So, we can say that

**"Hardware and software are complementary to each other."**

Computer software

Software helps us accomplish various tasks. You can write letters, make presentations, play games, etc., with the help of software.

## Types of Software

There are mainly two types of software:

1. Operating System Software

2. Application Software

# OPERATING SYSTEM SOFTWARE

An operating system is a software that acts as a middleman between the user and the computer system. It is the first software which has to be installed on the computer.

An operating system manages the operations of different input, output and storage devices of the computer.

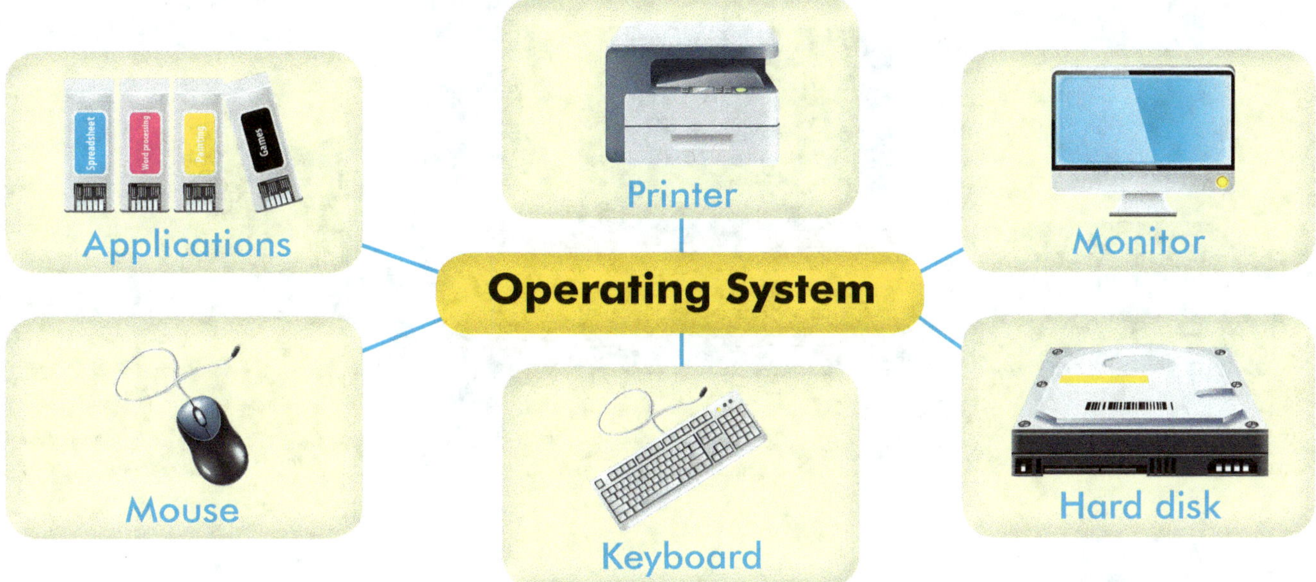


Without an operating system, a computer is merely a dumb machine. For example, you have a car which has petrol, engine, wheels, etc., but no driver to drive it. The car cannot move without a driver; it seems merely a dumb machine. Hence, a driver is the operating system for the car. In the same way, we need an operating system to run the computer.

There are different types of operating systems available in the market, such as:

Operating systems for your smartsphones and tablets are —

Android    iOS

**Do you know** ❓

*Google's Android is the most popular operating system used in smartphones and tablets. More than 2.5 billion people use the Android Operating System.*

## Functions of Operating System

The operating system controls all the components of a computer.

**Control Hardware**: One of the major functions of an operating system is to control the workings of different hardware devices attached to the computer and help them to work smoothly and efficiently.

**Run Software**: An operating system also helps the other software to run efficiently.

**Managing Information**: An operating system provides ways to store, manage and organize information on a computer.

**Booting**: It is one of the major functions of an operating system. Booting is the process of starting and restarting the computer. Booting is of two types: Cold booting and Warm booting.

**Cold Boot**: When a computer is switched On, this process of booting is called Cold Boot.

**Warm Boot**: The process to restart the computer that is already powered on is called Warm Boot. You can perform a warm boot by pressing the Control, Alt and Delete keys simultaneously or you can press a small restart button on the system unit.

# APPLICATION SOFTWARE

A set of instructions specially written to perform a particular task in a computer is known as Application software.

For example, a word processing is a program specially designed to create documents such as letters. A graphics program is specially designed to make drawings and images on the computer.

## Types of Application Software

There are many types of application software available in computer stores. Some are given below:

### Word Processing Software

These are the software specially designed to prepare notes, letters, official documents, etc. Microsoft Word, WordPad, etc. are some of the examples of word processing software.

### Spreadsheet

You can perform calculations, analyze data and present information with the help of spreadsheet software. The most commonly used spreadsheet program is Microsoft Excel.

### Database

Database allows you to manage a large collection of information in organized manner. The most widely used database program is Microsoft Access.

### Graphics Software

These software let you draw pictures, images, shapes and drawings on the computer easily and quickly. Paint, CorelDraw, Photoshop are some of the examples of graphics software.

## Games Software

Games software are used for entertainment. You can use games software to play games on the computer, like Pinball, Car Racing, etc.

## OPERATOR OF COMPUTER

### User

Users are the persons who communicate with computers and use the information generated by them. Users can be categorized as:

User

⇒ **Programmers**: The persons who write sets of instructions to design particular software are called programmers. The process of writing these instructions (program) is called programming.

⇒ **Operators**: The persons who use the different software to do different types of work on the computer are called operators. They also know how to operate these software.

### LET'S HAVE A LOOK

- A computer is an electronic machine which consists of various parts.

- A computer works with the help of these parts known as its components.

- Hardware is the part of the computer which can be touched and seen.

- Software are the hidden parts of the computer that cannot be touched.

- Software is a set of instructions that instruct hardware what to do.

- Hardware and software are complementary to each other.

- There are two main types of software: Operating System Software and Application Software.

- An operating system is a software which acts as a middleman between the user and the computer system.

- An application software is a program that performs specific tasks for users.

## BRAIN TEASER

**1.   Write the answers to the following questions:**

a.   Name the two components of the computer.

b.   What is hardware?

c.   What is software?

d.   "Hardware and software are complementary to each other." How?

e.   What is an operating system software?

f.   List any two functions of an operating system.

g.   Differentiate between cold boot and warm boot.

h.   Define users.

## 2.   Name the following:

a.   Different hardware components

b.   Two types of software

c.   Two types of booting

d.   Two examples of operating system software

e .   Two types of application software

## 3.   Multiple Choice Questions
Tick (✓) the correct answer:

a.   A type of hardware
   i.   Windows    ☐    ii.  Paint    ☐    iii.  Keyboard

b.   An operating system software
   i.   Windows    ☐      ii.  Games
   iii.  Word processor    ☐

c. An application software

    i.   Booting ☐     ii.  UNIX ☐

    iii. Word Processor ☐

d. Graphics software

    i.   MS-Word ☐   ii.  Paint ☐   iii.  Media Player ☐

e. Process of starting and restarting the computer

    i.   Turning ON ☐   ii.  Booting ☐   iii.  Starting ☐

f. A person who writes a set of instructions for the computer

    i.   User ☐   ii.  Operator ☐   iii.  Programmer ☐

## 4. Write 'T' for true and 'F' for false in the boxes:

a. You cannot touch hardware. ☐

b. Keyboard and monitor are the hardware components. ☐

c. Softwares are the hidden parts of the computer. ☐

d. Windows is an example of application software. ☐

e. Word processing is used to create drawings. ☐

f. The process of starting and restarting the computer is called booting. ☐

## 5. Fill in the blanks:

a. An ________________________ is a software which acts as a middleman between users and computers.

b. ________________________ and ________________________ are the two components of the computer system.

c. Hardware defines the parts of the computer which can be ________________________ and ________________________ .

d. ________________________ is a set of programs specially written to perform a particular task.

e. ________________________ software is used to calculate and analyze data.

# Cross every third letter and write below what you get:

**S O L F T G W A K R E**

<br>

**O P S E R G A T M I N S G**
**S Y W S T N E M**

<br>

**W I S N D G O W M S**

<br>

**A P S P L G I C M A T S I O S N**
**S O A F T B W A Q R E**

**Solve the Crossword Puzzle:**

a.   An input device

b.   A storage device

c.   A part of CPU

d.   An output device

e.   An operating system software

f.   Process of starting and restarting the computer

g.   An application software

h.   A set of instructions

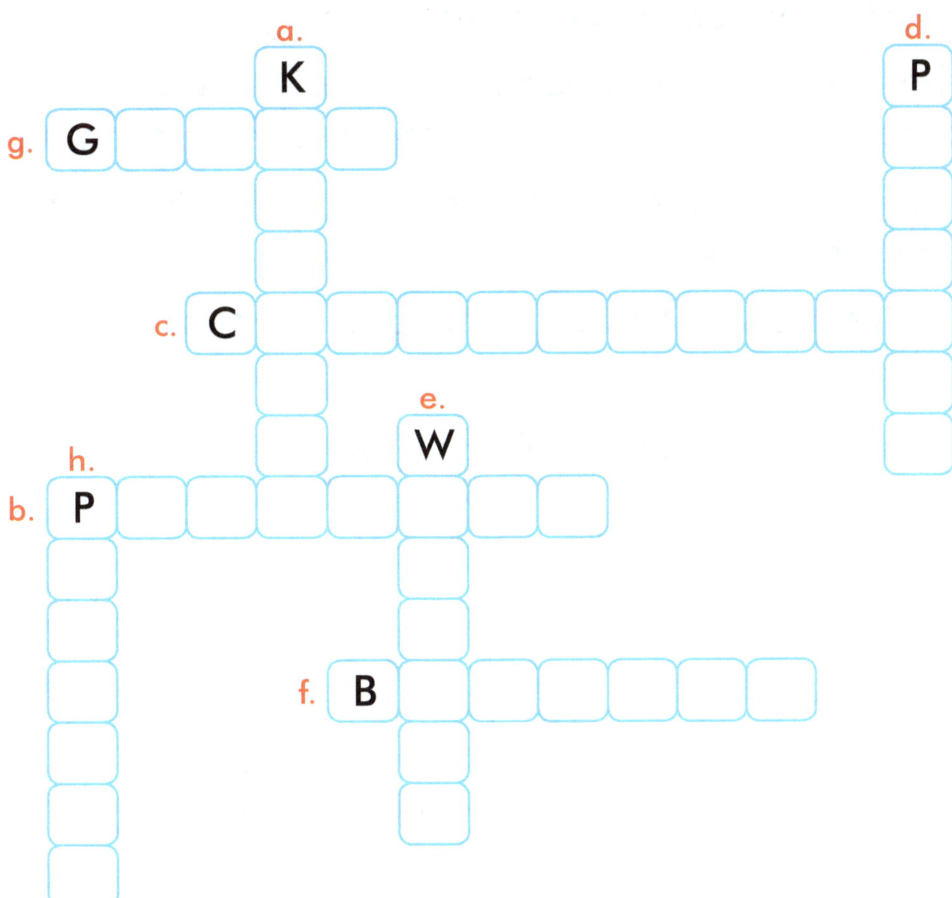

# 3 Computer Memory

## COMPUTER MEMORY

**Memory** plays a very important role in a computer. It is a storage area which is used to store data, instructions and information.

Memory holds both the data that needs to be processed, and the data that has already been processed by the **CPU** (Central Processing Unit).

Computer memory is the place where a computer holds current programs and the programs that are in use.

In a computer, there are two types of computer memory: Primary memory and Secondary memory.

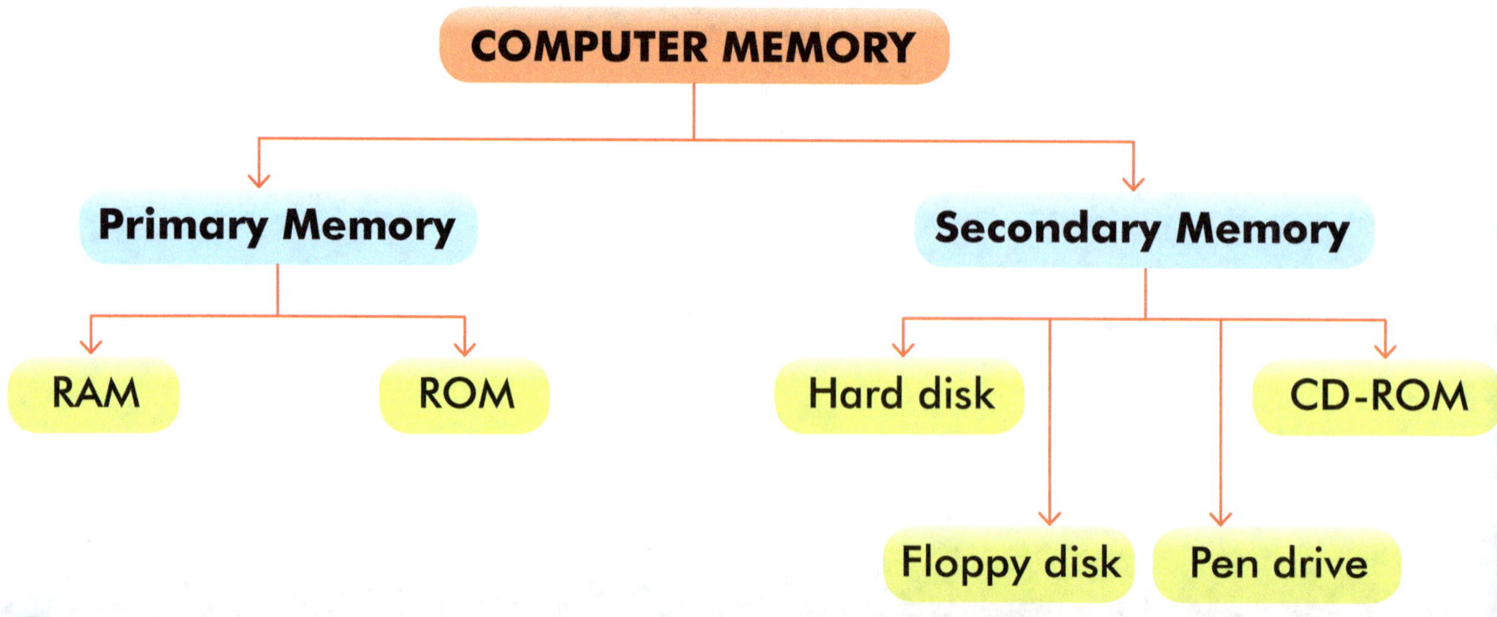

## PRIMARY MEMORY

Primary Memory is also called Internal Memory or Main Memory. It is an electronic memory which looks like an Electronic Chip. This chip is fixed on the motherboard.

Whatever data you enter into the computer, that data is first sent to the Primary memory. The CPU can process only the data that is in the Primary memory. Two types of Primary memory are RAM and ROM.

## RAM

RAM stands for Random Access Memory. It is also called Read/Write Memory. The CPU (Central Processing Unit) and other devices can read the data from RAM and also write the data onto RAM.

RAM is volatile memory. This memory contains the data until the power is supplied to it. When power supply is OFF, all the data in this memory will be erased. That means, RAM is the temporary storage memory. For this reason, you must save all items you may need in the future. Saving is the process of copying data from RAM to the Hard disk.

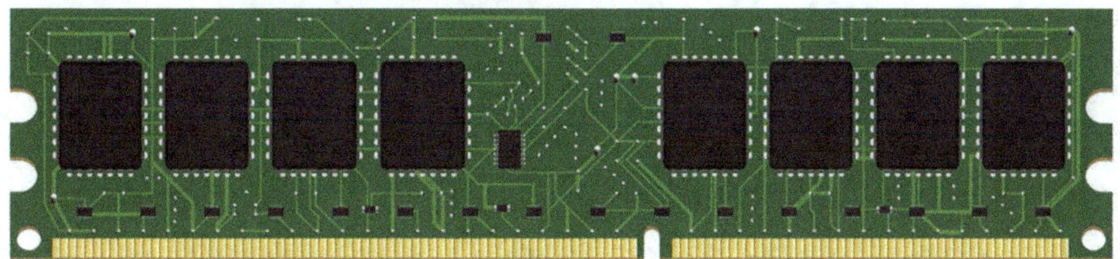

RAM

## ROM

ROM stands for Read Only Memory. ROM is the permanent storage medium. It contains the data which is the permanent part of the memory. Users can only read the data from this memory. It is not possible to write the data on to ROM.

ROM

## SECONDARY MEMORY

Secondary Memory is also called External Memory. Sometimes, a program is so large that it is not possible to store that data in the Primary Memory (because the Primary Memory has limited storage capacity). So, in that case, it is needed to store the portion of that data on the Primary Memory and the remaining on the Secondary Memory.

It is called External Memory because it is externally attached to the computer and stores the data permanently. The data saved in the secondary memory is not lost when power supply is disconnected from the computer.

The different secondary memory devices such as hard disk drive, floppy disk, CD/DVD-ROM, pen drive, etc., are used in the computer.

Floppy disk

Hard disk

CD-ROM

Pen drive

You have already studied about them in the previous chapter.

## STORAGE UNITS

As everything has its measuring units such as liquid is measured in litre (l) or millilitre (ml); solid is measured in gram (g) or kilogram (kg). Similarly, computer memory can also be measured. It is measured in Bits and Bytes.

## BIT

A bit is the smallest unit of data in a computer. Bits mean Binary Digits in the form of 0 and 1. A computer does not understand the other languages as we humans can. It can only understand the language of 0's and 1's that machine language consists of.

## Byte

A byte is a collection of 8 bits. In other words, a group of eight bits forms a single byte and a single byte represents a single character. That means, a single character needs one byte or 8 bits to store in memory.

In another words, byte is the smallest storage unit to store even a single character.

# Example:

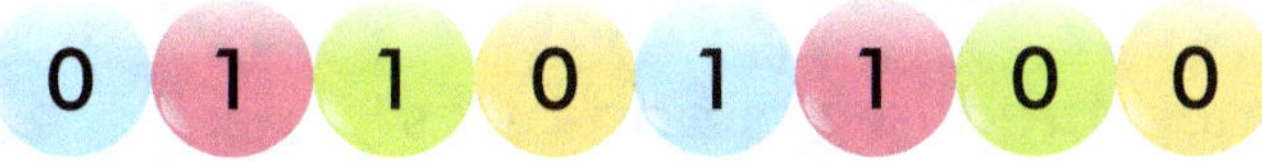



Here, we have 8 bits, which form 1 byte.

## Kilobyte (KB)

A Kilobyte consists of 1024 bytes. That means, 1 KB contains 1024 bytes, where 1 byte contains 8 bits, so 1 KB contains 8192 bits.

## Megabyte (MB)

A Megabyte is a collection of 1024 Kilobytes. That means, 1 MB contains 1024 KB.

## Gigabyte (GB)

A Gigabyte is a collection of 1024 Megabytes. That means, 1 GB contains 1024 MB.

**The table below shows the units of memory and its equivalents.**

| Bit | = | Smallest Unit |
| --- | --- | --- |
| Byte (B) | = | 8 Bits |
| Kilobyte (KB) | = | 1024 Bytes (about 1,024 characters) |
| Megabyte (MB) | = | 1024 Kilobytes (about 1,048,576 characters) |
| Gigabyte (GB) | = | 1024 Megabytes (about 1,073,741,824 characters) |

## LET'S HAVE A LOOK

- Memory is a storage area which is used to store data, instructions and information.
- Memory holds both the data that needs to be processed, and the data that has already been processed by the CPU.
- Primary Memory is also called Internal Memory or Main Memory.
- Two types of Primary memory are RAM and ROM.
- RAM stands for Random Access Memory. RAM is volatile memory.
- ROM stands for Read Only Memory.

- Secondary Memory is also called External Memory.
- Computer memory is measured in bits and bytes.
- A bit is the smallest unit of data in a computer.
- A byte is a collection of 8 bits.

## BRAIN TEASER

**1.  Answer the following questions:**

a.  Define computer memory.

b.  What are the measuring units of computer memory?

c.  Name the two types of computer memory.

d.  Name some of the secondary storage devices used in the computer

e.  Define bits and bytes.

f.  Write the full forms of RAM and ROM respectively.

2. **Write the difference between:**

a. **Primary Memory**                    **Secondary Memory**

_______________________           _______________________

_______________________           _______________________

_______________________           _______________________

_______________________           _______________________

b. **RAM**                              **ROM**

_______________________           _______________________

_______________________           _______________________

_______________________           _______________________

3. **Write 'T' for true and 'F' for false in the boxes:**

a. Computer memory is used to store data and instructions.

b. Computer memory is measured in gram and kilogram.

c. Primary memory is the external memory.

d. RAM is the main memory of the computer.

e. Hard disk is the example of secondary memory.

f. Saving is the process of copying data from RAM to the hard disk.

g. Computer memory is measured in bits and bytes.

h. One byte consists of eight bits.

4. **Fill in the blanks:**

a. _______________________ plays a very important role in a computer.

b. Primary memory is also called _______________________ memory.

c. RAM is also called _______________________ memory.

d.    ROM stands for ___________________.

e.    Computer memory is measured in _________________ and
      _________________.

f.    A byte is a collection of _________________ bits.

## 5.    Multiple Choice Questions
**Tick (✓) the correct answer:**

a.    Primary memory is also called

    i.    Main memory ☐        ii.    ROM ☐

    iii.   External memory ☐

b.    Volatile memory

    i.    RAM ☐        ii.  ROM ☐        iii.  BYTE ☐

c.    The smallest unit of information which a computer can process

    i.   Bit ☐        ii.  Byte ☐        iii.  MHZ ☐

d.    One Kilobyte is equal to

    i.    1024 bytes ☐        ii.  1024 MB ☐        iii.  1024 GB ☐

e.    One Gigabyte is equal to

    i.    1024 MB ☐        ii.  1024 TB ☐        iii.  1024 B ☐

## 6.    Match the following:

| | | |
|---|---|---|
| a. | 1 Bit | 1 Kilobyte |
| b. | 8 Bits | 1 Megabyte |
| c. | 1024 Bytes | Smallest Unit |
| d. | 1024 Kilobytes | 1 Gigabyte |
| e. | 1024 Megabytes | 1 Byte |

# 4 Windows Operating System

Hey friends! We learnt about operating system software in the second chapter. Now, in this chapter we will study about one of the operating systems, *i.e.* Windows 10.

## WINDOWS

Operating System (OS) is used to control the functions of the computer system. Windows is the most important operating system nowadays.

Windows Operating system was developed by Microsoft Corporation in the year 1983. It is based on Graphical User Interface (GUI) in which information is represented in graphical ways.

When you start the computer, operating system is the first software that loads into the memory of the computer, called booting. While your computer is booting, a picture of Windows flag is displayed on the monitor.

The owner of Microsoft is Bill Gates.

## Various Versions of Windows

Various forms of MS-Windows are called versions.

Windows has various versions like Windows 95, Windows 98, Windows XP, Windows Vista, Windows 7, Windows 8 and Windows 10. In this chapter, we will study about Windows 10.

## WINDOWS 10

Windows 10 is the lastest updated operating system from Microsoft. It controls the overall activity of your computer and ensures that all parts of your computer work smoothly.

It is a **GUI** (**Graphical User Interface**) based operating system in which all the items are represented in the form of pictures and graphical links. The commands are operated with the help of the **mouse** instead of using the keyboard.

Windows 10 is used for both home and business purposes.

## STARTING WINDOWS 10 (Cold Boot)

**Switch On** the computer; **Windows** starts **automatically** and a **Welcome screen** appears.

You may be asked to enter the **password**. You can ask your teacher the password.

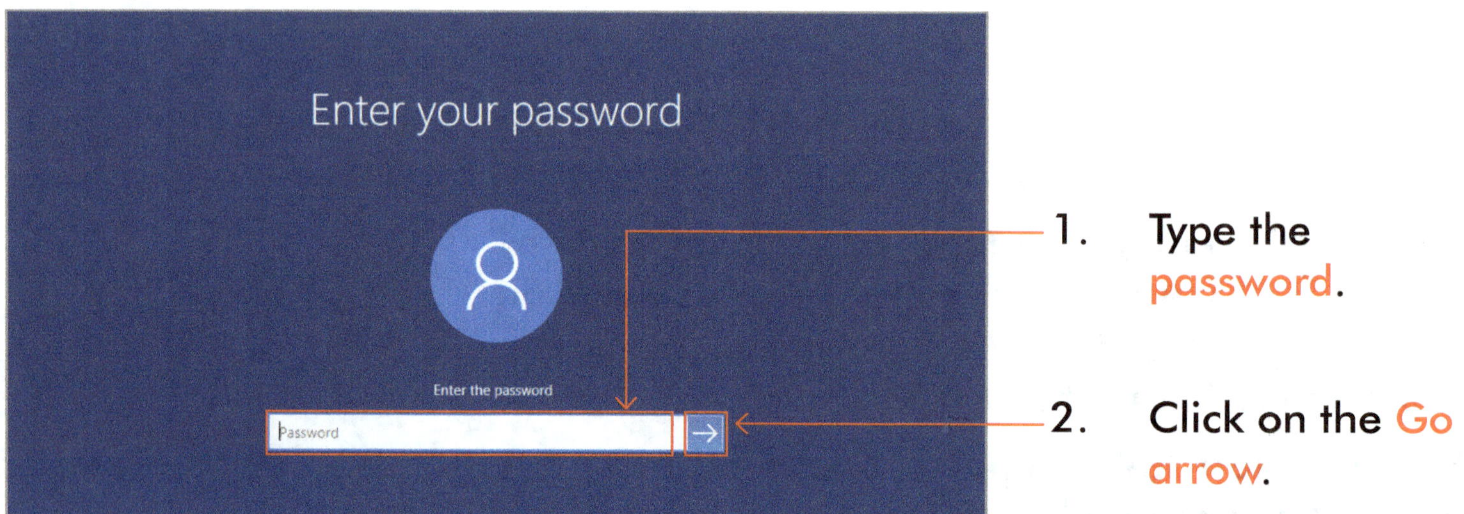


1. Type the **password**.

2. Click on the **Go arrow**.

Now, you will get the final **desktop screen**.

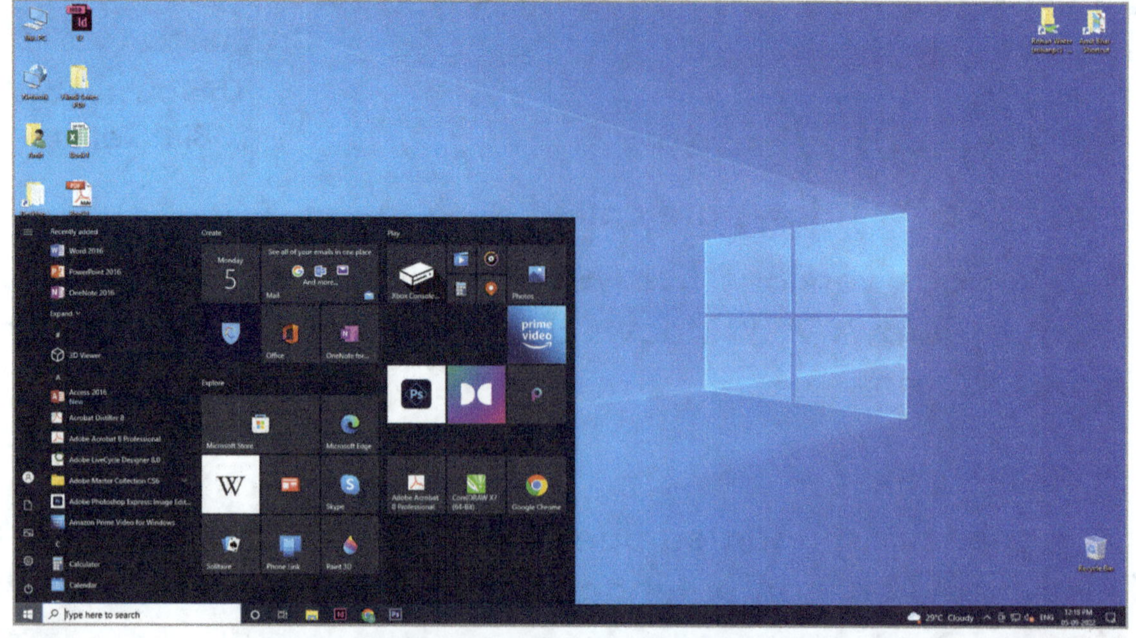

Your computer is now ready to work.

# WINDOWS 10 DESKTOP SCREEN

**Desktop** is the first screen that appears when you turn on the computer screen. You will see the following items:

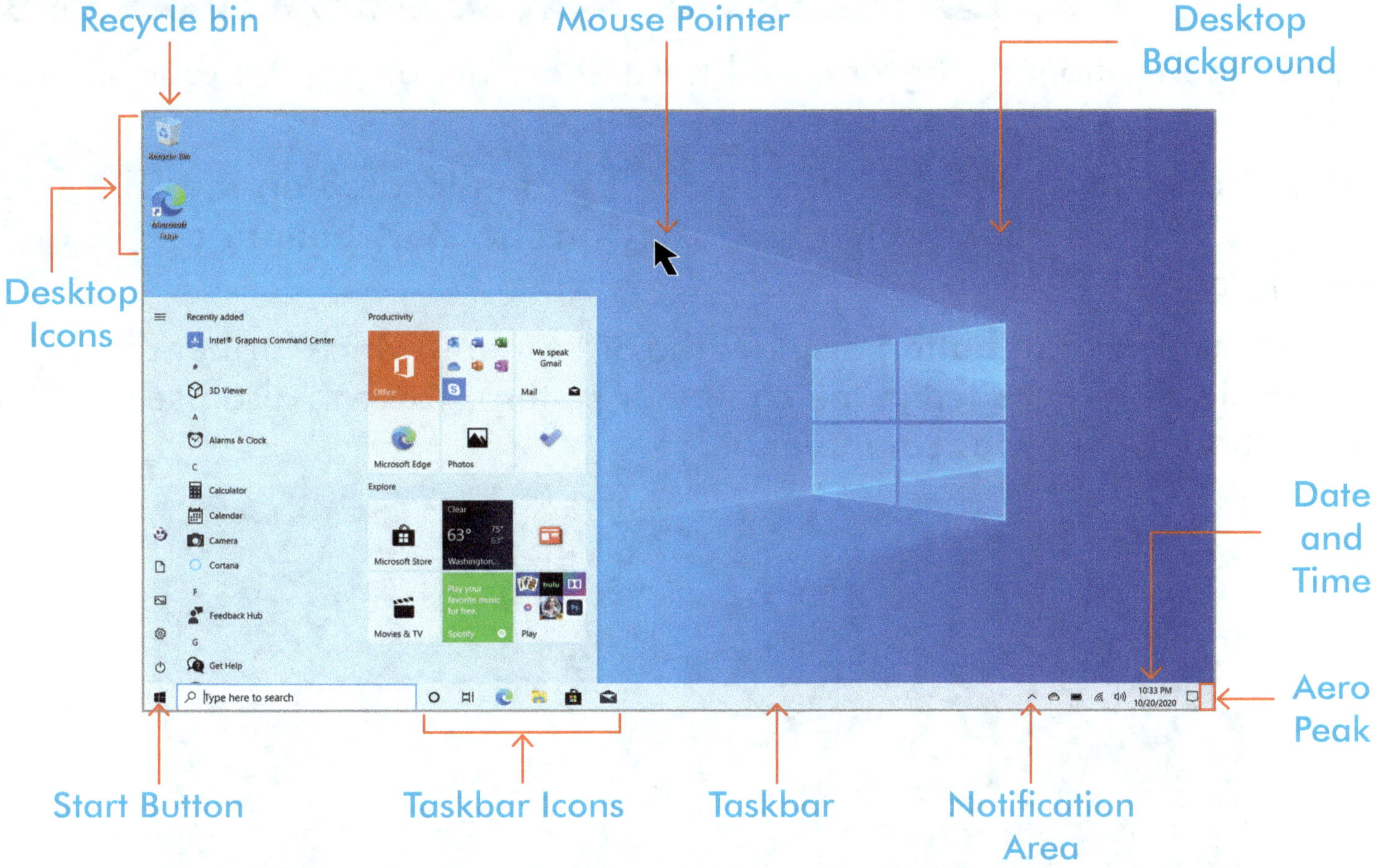

**Desktop Background**: The background picture of Windows 10 desktop is known as Desktop Background. Various options are available for desktop background in Windows 10. You can set the desktop background on your computer as per your choice.

**Recycle Bin**: When you delete a file, it is moved to the Recycle bin. This allows you to recover the file later on.

**Desktop Icons**: An icon is a small picture on the desktop which is used to open a program, file or folder. Some of the desktop icons are shown below:

This PC      Recycle Bin      Document      Microsoft Edge      Network

**Taskbar**: The taskbar is a long bar at the bottom of the desktop. It contains Start button at the left corner and clock at the right corner. When you open a program file, it appears on the taskbar.

**Taskbar Icons**: Some programs will have shortcuts on the taskbar for easy access.

**Start Button**: Start button is a box-shaped button located on the left corner of the taskbar. When you click on the start button, a menu appears.

**Start Menu**: The Start button displays the Start menu which further displays a list of applications installed in the computer system. You can also use the Start menu to Shut Down your computer.

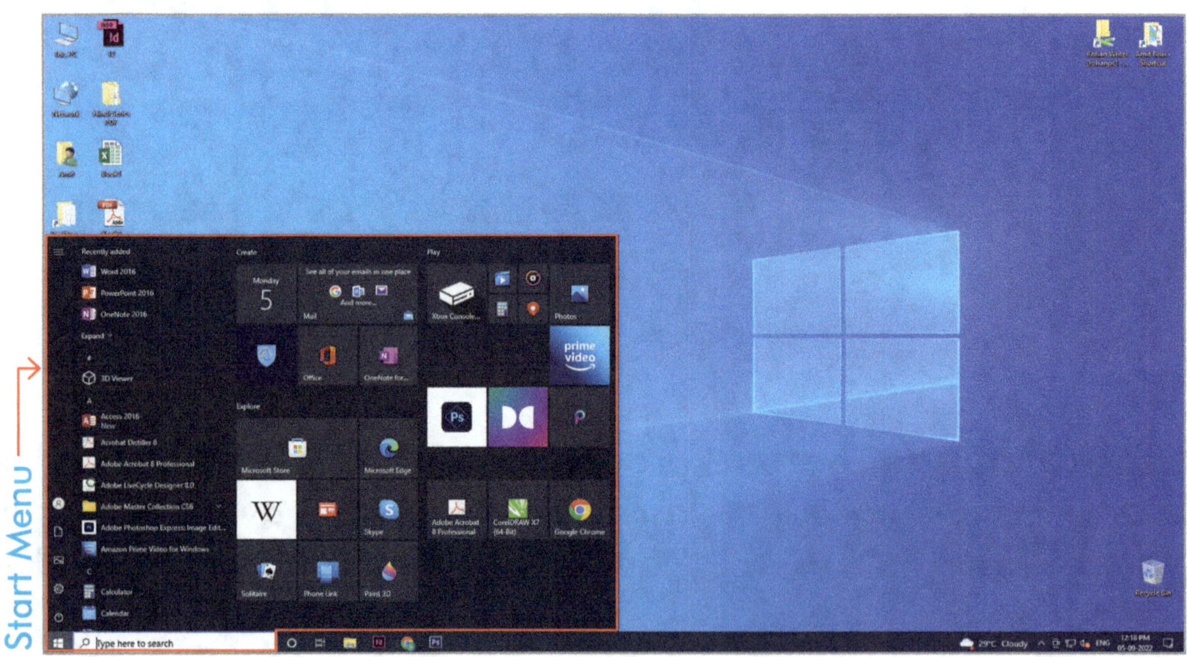

**Time and Date**: On the right corner of the taskbar, you can see the current Time and Date on your computer. Click on the Time and Date area to see the full Time and Date box. You can also change Time and Date of computer.

**Notification Area**: This area displays small icons that notify you about the things that currently happen on the computer.

**Mouse Pointer**: It is a small arrow on the computer screen, which helps to point, click or double-click the various items on the desktop.

**Pinning**: Pinning is a great way to add shortcuts to your most often used programs in Windows 10. You can pin items to the Taskbar at the bottom of the screen or to the Start menu. That saves a lot of clicks and makes you more efficient.

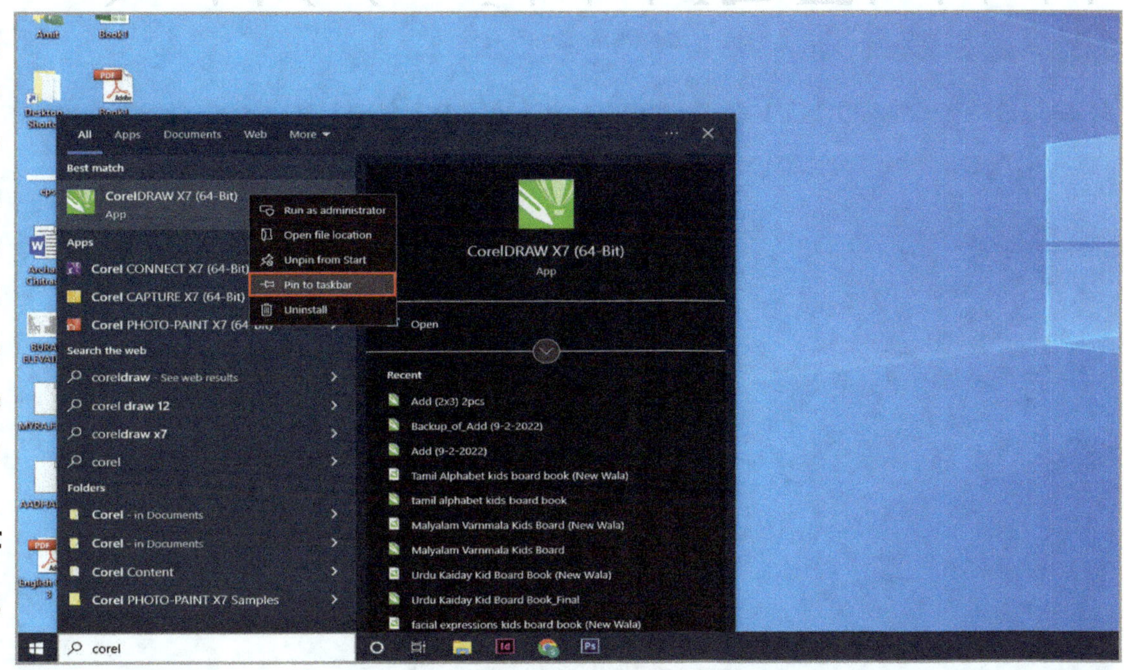

**Jump List**: A jump list is a system-provided menu that appears when the user right-clicks a program in the taskbar or on the Start menu. It is used to provide quick access to recently or frequently-used documents. For example, a Microsoft Word jump list might display all the recent documents opened.

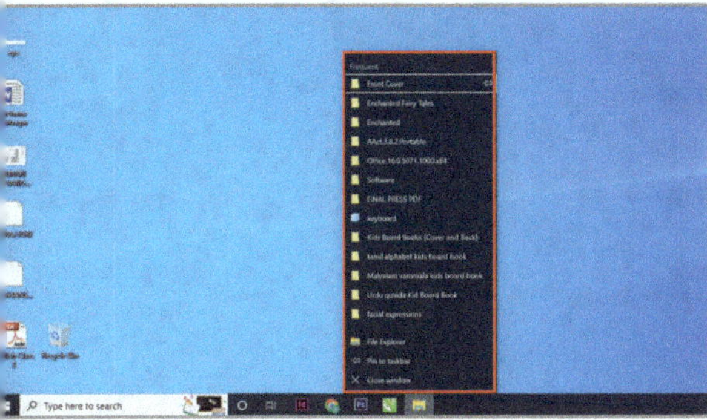

**Gadgets**: Gadgets are small programs designed for a specialised purpose. Some of the gadgets are Clock, Calendar, Games, Slide Show and Feed headlines.

**Aero Peek**: In the far right corner of the taskbar, there is the Aero Peek button. When you click or point over with the mouse on Aero Peek, it displays the desktop by turning all windows transparent.

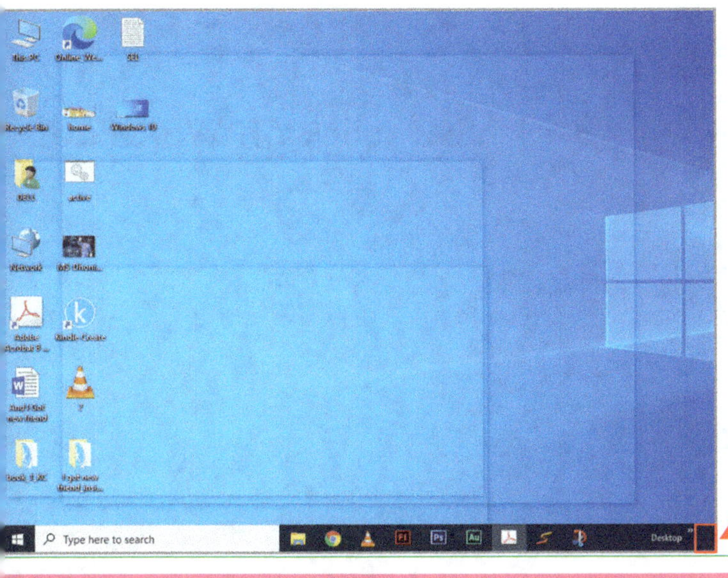

#  OPENING A PROGRAM

You can now open a program (WordPad) in the computer.

1. Click on the **Start** button.

2. Click on **Windows Accessories**.

3. Now, click on **WordPad**.

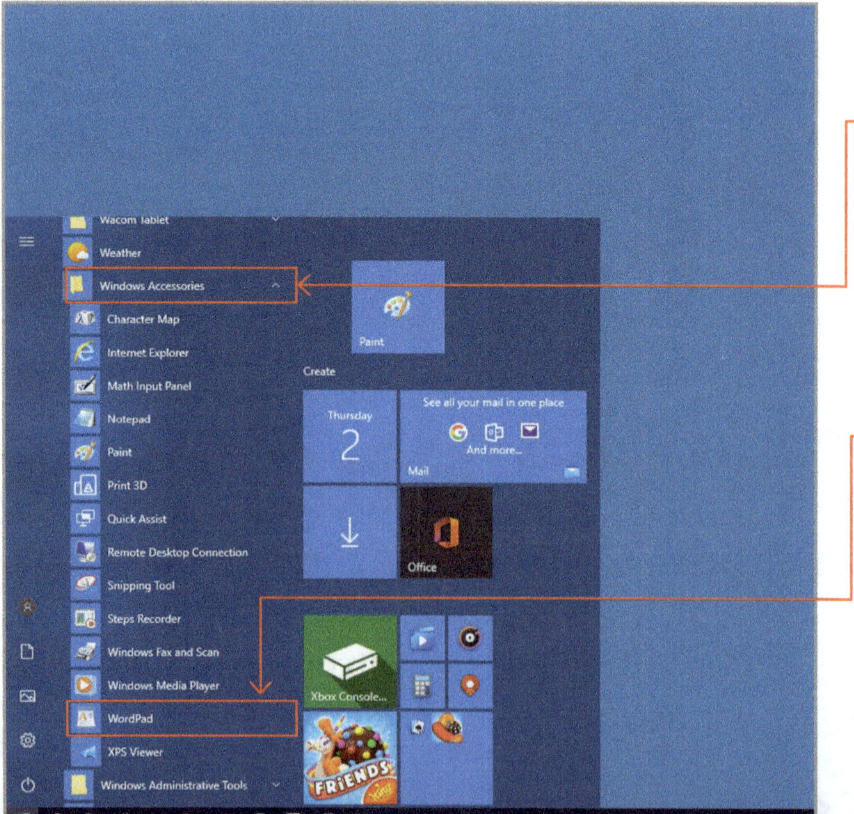

The WordPad application will appear in front of you.

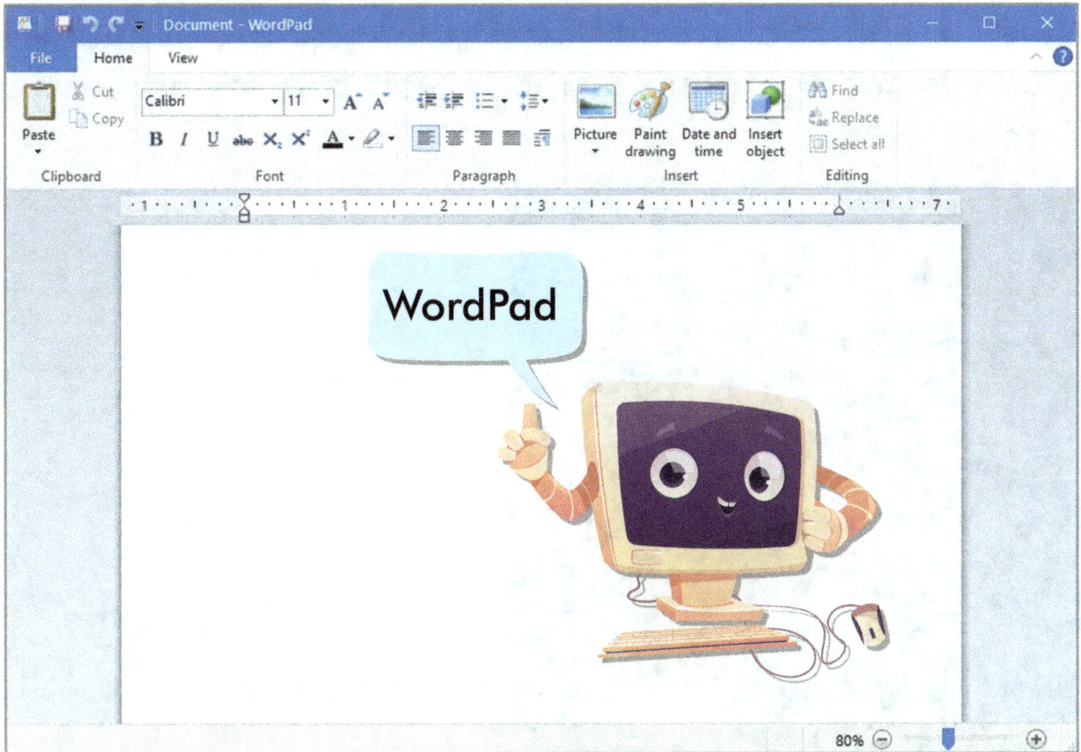


You can now work on it.

## CLOSING THE PROGRAM

After finishing your work on the computer, you can close the program by clicking on the cross ( × ) on the right corner.

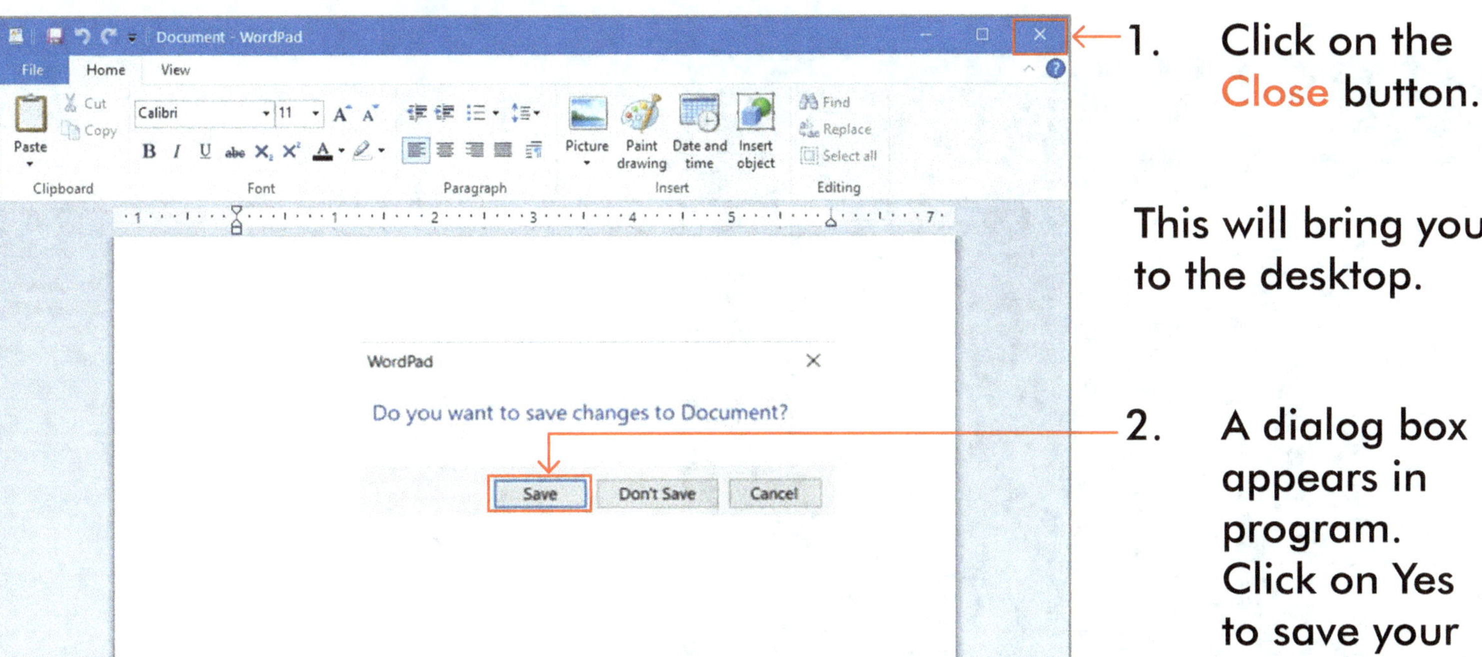


1. Click on the Close button.

   This will bring you to the desktop.

2. A dialog box appears in program. Click on Yes to save your document.

We must close all the programs to free up the space of the hard disk.

# RESTARTING THE COMPUTER (Warm Boot)

Restarting Windows shuts down and starts up your computer again immediately. If your computer is not operating properly, you can restart your computer to fix the problem.

1. Click on the Start button. The start menu will appear.

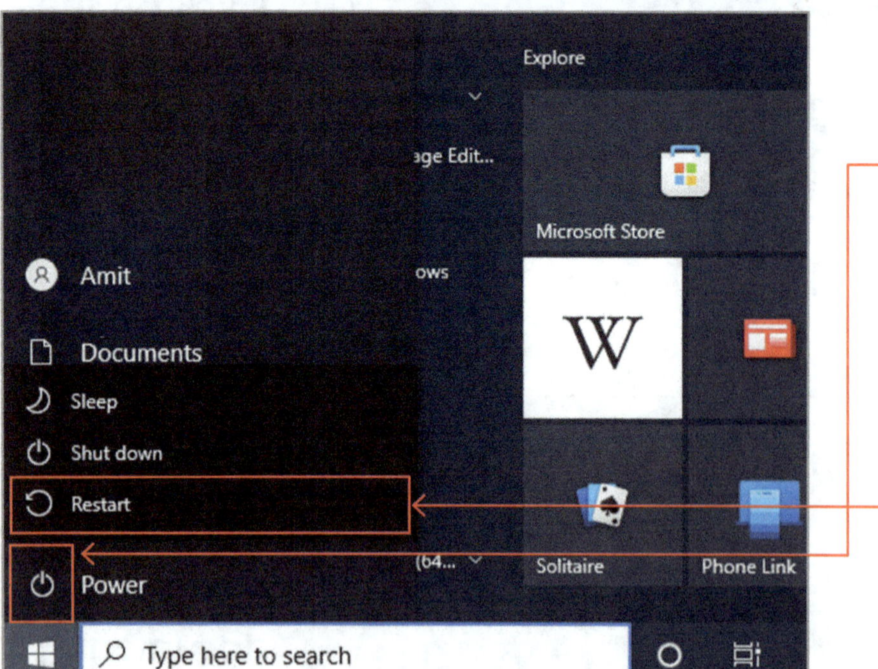

2. Click on Power button. A menu will appear.

3. Click on Restart.

Windows shuts down and your computer restarts.

# SHUTTING DOWN THE COMPUTER

After completing your work, you need to switch off your computer.

To shut down a computer properly, follow the given steps:

1.   Click on the Start button. The start menu will appear.

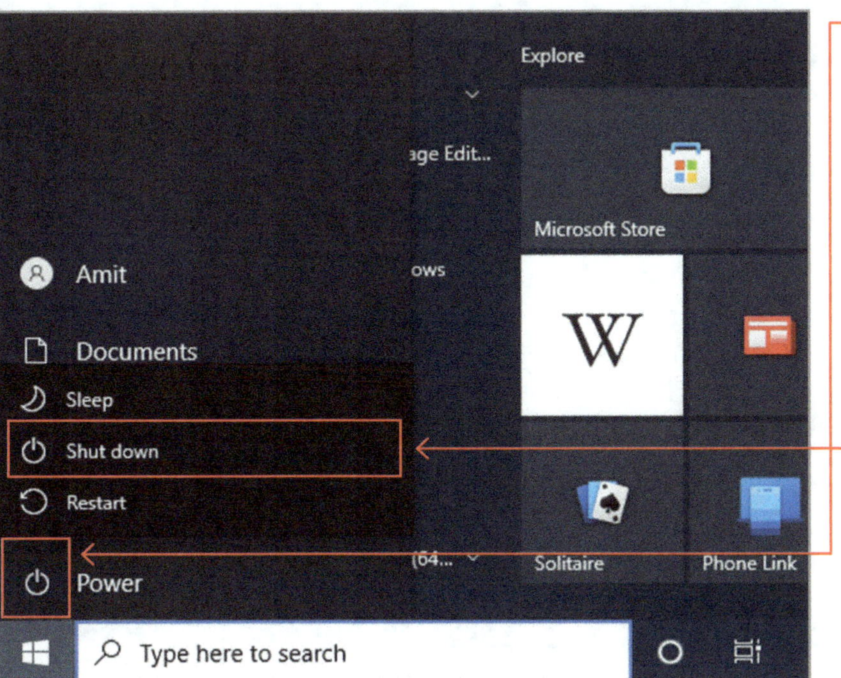

2.   Click on Power button. A menu will appear.

3.   Click on Shut Down.

Windows 10 shuts down and turns off the computer.

## LET'S HAVE A LOOK

- Operating System (OS) is used to control the functions of the computer system.
- Windows is the most important operating system nowadays.
- Windows Operating system was developed by Microsoft Corporation in the year 1983.
- Windows 10 is the latest updated operating system from Microsoft.
- Windows 10 is used for both home and business purposes.
- When you delete a file, it is moved to the Recycle bin.
- An icon is a small picture on the desktop.
- The taskbar is a long bar at the bottom of the desktop.
- Start button is a box-shaped button located on the left corner of the taskbar.
- Gadgets are small programs designed for a specialised purpose.

## BRAIN TEASER

**1. Write the answers to the following questions:**

a.  What is an operating system?

b.  What is Windows 10?

c.  What is Desktop background?

d.  What is the use of the taskbar?

e.  What is Start Menu?

f.  What is a gadget?

**2.  Write the use of each of the following:**

a.  Recycle Bin

b.  Aero Peek

c.  Icons

d.  Jump List

e.  Pinning

3. **Multiple Choice Questions**

   **Tick (✓) the correct answer:**

   a.   A small arrow on the screen

   i.   Mouse ☐   ii.   Mouse pointer ☐   iii.   Icon ☐

   b.   The small picture or graphics on the desktop screen

   i.   Start menu ☐   ii.   Windows ☐   iii.   Icons ☐

   c.   On which operating system is Windows 10 based?

   i.   GUI ☐   ii.   CUI ☐   iii.   EUI ☐

   d.   All deleted files go to

   i.   Desktop ☐   ii.   Folder ☐   iii.   Recycle bin ☐

   e.   The long bar at the bottom of the screen

   i.   Taskbar ☐   ii.   Start button ☐   iii.   Start menu ☐

   f.   A box-shaped button located on the left corner of the taskbar

   i.   Mouse ☐   ii.   Start button ☐   iii.   Start menu ☐

4. **Fill in the blanks:**

   a.   _________________ is used for both home and business purposes.

   b.   Small symbols or pictures on the desktop are called _________________.

   c.   The _________________ is a long bar at the bottom of the desktop.

   d.   _________________ is the box-shaped button at the bottom left corner.

   e.   _________________ are small programs designed for a specialised purpose.

5. **Write 'T' for true and 'F' for false in the boxes:**

   a.   Windows is an application software. ☐

   b.   The small arrow present on the desktop is called Icon. ☐

   c.   Windows 10 was developed by Microsoft. ☐

**Find out the names of the different components of Windows 10 screen:**

| A | Z | Q | N | S | P | G | W | X | I | Z | K | L | R | Q |
|---|---|---|---|---|---|---|---|---|---|---|---|---|---|---|
| B | U | S | T | Q | F | P | N | G | C | H | D | R | G | Z |
| R | W | T | S | D | E | S | K | T | O | P | G | S | N | X |
| W | R | A | V | T | X | A | R | D | N | C | K | T | X | W |
| N | G | R | Z | O | D | C | Z | Q | S | B | Y | A | E | R |
| I | N | T | Q | M | C | B | F | S | A | G | U | R | S | I |
| P | J | B | F | R | L | Y | D | R | B | K | T | T | M | Y |
| M | U | U | L | P | O | I | N | T | E | R | L | M | E | L |
| F | Y | T | Q | F | C | H | K | P | M | N | R | E | N | N |
| W | T | T | N | T | K | L | I | S | K | O | P | N | E | A |
| E | Q | O | F | C | G | Q | N | L | H | C | Q | U | I | V |
| M | A | N | O | T | I | F | I | C | A | T | I | O | N | E |



Start your computer in the computer lab and identify the various components present on the desktop.

Draw the symbols of any three icons that you see on the screen of Windows 10. Also, name the icons.

# Formative Assessment-2
## (Chapters 3-4)

**1.    Complete the table:**

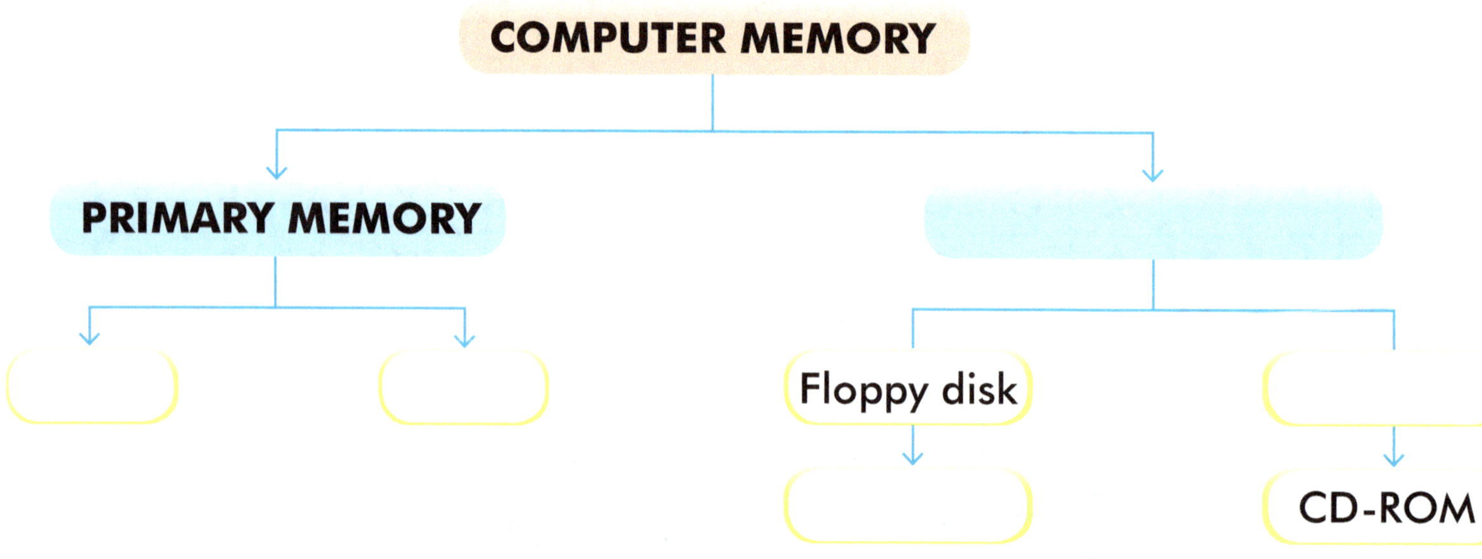


**2.    Label the following Windows 10 screen:**

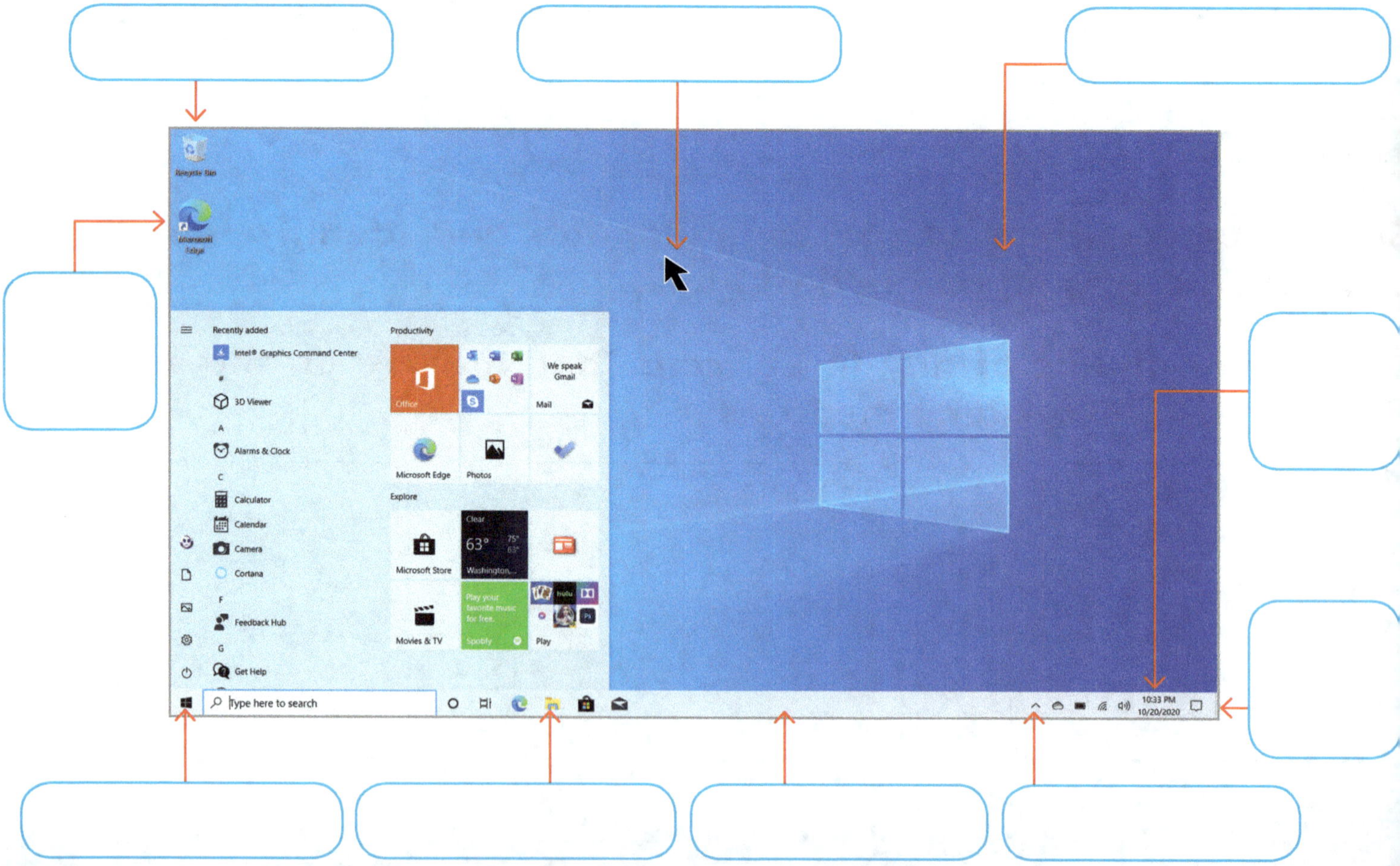

**1. Answer the following:**

a. What is a computer?

b. What are the four main jobs of a computer?

c. Differentiate between:

    i. Input devices and output devices

    ii. RAM and ROM

    iii. Hardware and Software

d. What are the different functions of an operating system?

e. What is Application software?

f. What is main memory?

g. What are icons?

**2. Name the following:**

a. Any two input devices

b. Any two storage devices

c. The parts of CPU

d. Any two output devices

e. Two types of software

f. Any two Application softwares

**3. Fill in the blanks:**

a. The mouse is an _________________ device.　　(input / output)

b. The monitor is a _________________.　　(hardware / software)

c. The hard disk is a _________________ device. (processing / storage)

d. Windows 10 is an _________________.

    (Operating System / Application Software)

e. ROM is _________________ memory.　　(Primary / Secondary)

4. **Write 'YES' or 'NO':**

   a.    Is the keyboard hardware?                              _______________

   b.    Is the pen drive an input device?                      _______________

   c.    Is RAM primary memory?                                 _______________

   d.    Is MS-Word an operating system?                        _______________

   e.    Can you touch hardware?                                _______________

   f.    Is the CD-ROM secondary memory?                        _______________

   g.    Is 1 byte = 8 bits?                                    _______________

5. **Tick (✓) the correct answer:**

   a.    Entering data or instructions into the computer is called

         i.   Output ☐          ii.  Input ☐          iii.  Process ☐

   b.    An arrow moves when you move the mouse

         i.   Insertion Point ☐    ii.  Cursor ☐

         iii. Mouse Pointer ☐

   c.    Restarting the computer is known as

         i.   Cold boot ☐        ii.  Warm boot ☐      iii.  Opening ☐

   d.    We can touch and feel

         i.   Hardware ☐         ii.  Software ☐        iii.  Both ☐

   e.    A box button at the bottom left corner of the taskbar

         i.   Start Menu ☐       ii.  Icon ☐            iii.  Start button ☐

6. **Match the following:**

   a.    Processing Device            i.    Long bar at the bottom of screen

   b.    Hard disk                    ii.   CPU

   c.    Booting                      iii.  Storage device

   d.    Taskbar                      iv.   Starting the computer

# Features in Paint

**Before moving ahead, let us first review a little we did earlier.**

## PAINT

As you all must be remembering, Paint is a simple graphics program in which you can draw and colour different images and shapes using different tools given in it. These tools are line tool, curve tool, polygon tool, oval tool, pencil tool and many others.

## Starting Paint Program

Follow these steps to open the Paint program:

1. Click on Start button.

2. Click on Windows Accessories.

3. Click on Paint.

The Paint program will appear on the desktop.

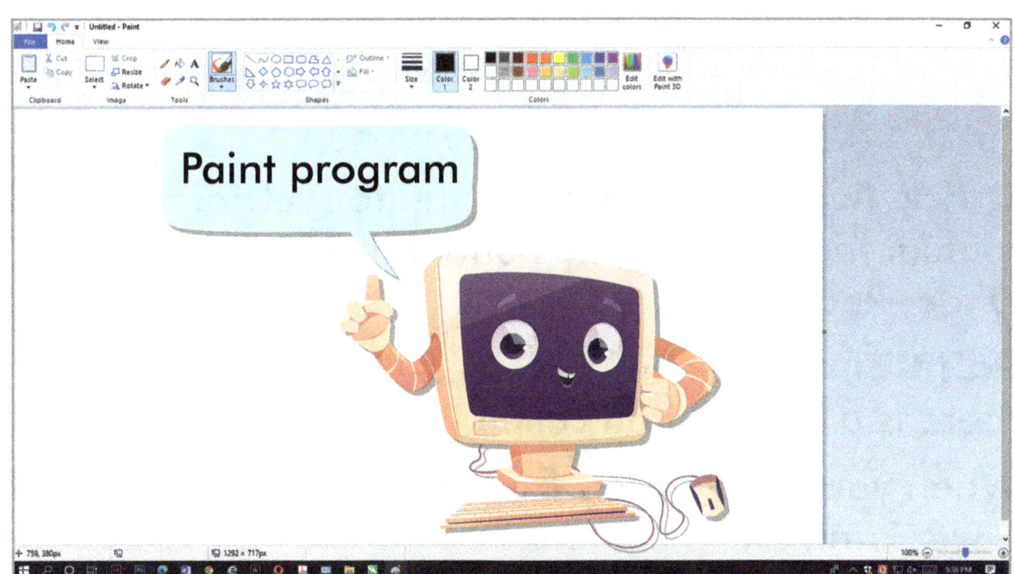

## COMPONENTS OF PAINT WINDOW

In Windows 10, you will see that Paint is completely modified as compared to the old version of Paint, but it is almost similar to Windows 7. Just have a look.

Old Version Paint (Windows 7)

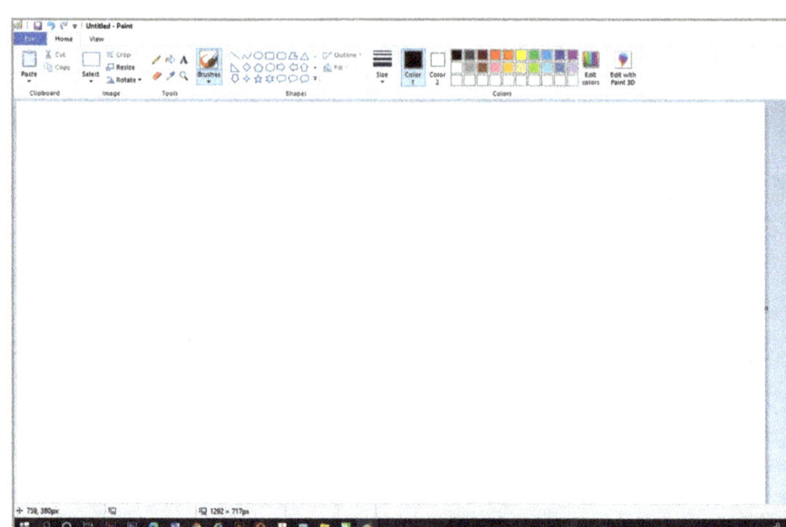

New Version Paint (Windows 10)

Now, in the new version, all the items are at the top of the window.

Let's have a look at the different components of a Paint window.

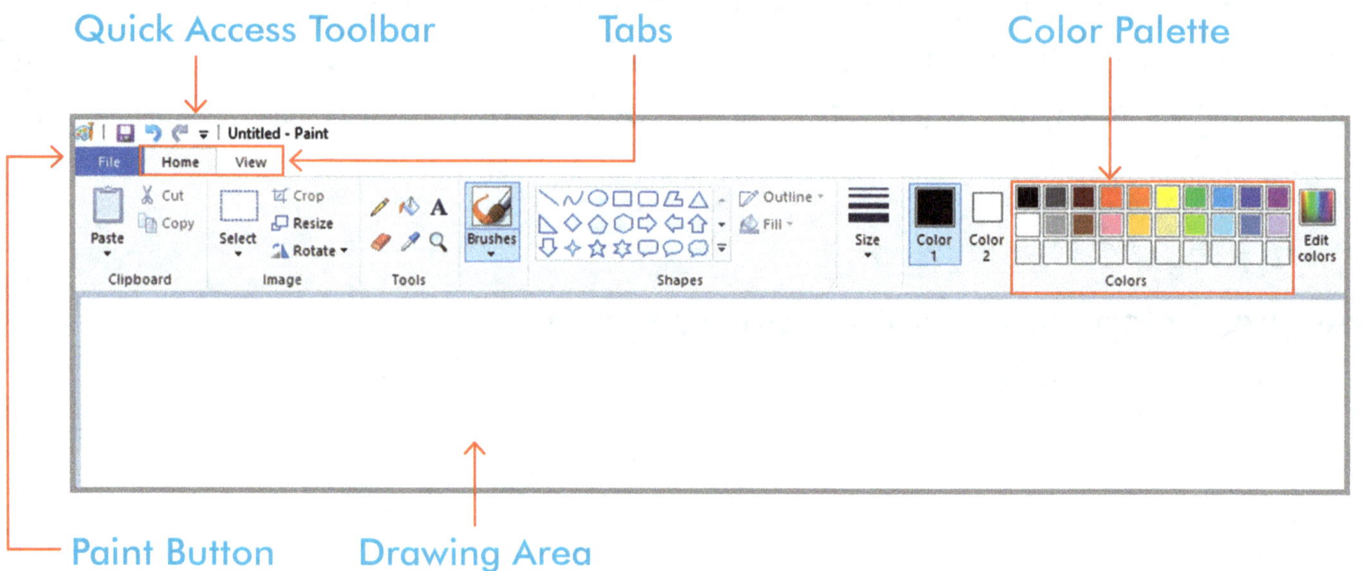


**Quick Access Toolbar**: On the top left of the Paint window, there is a small toolbar that contains the buttons like Save, Undo, Redo, etc.

**Paint Button**: Below the Quick Access Toolbar and on the left side, there is a blue button called Paint Button.

When you click on this button, you will see a list of options like New, Open, Save, Print, etc.

**TABS**: Next to Paint button, there are two tabs — Home Tab and View Tab —in the Paint window.

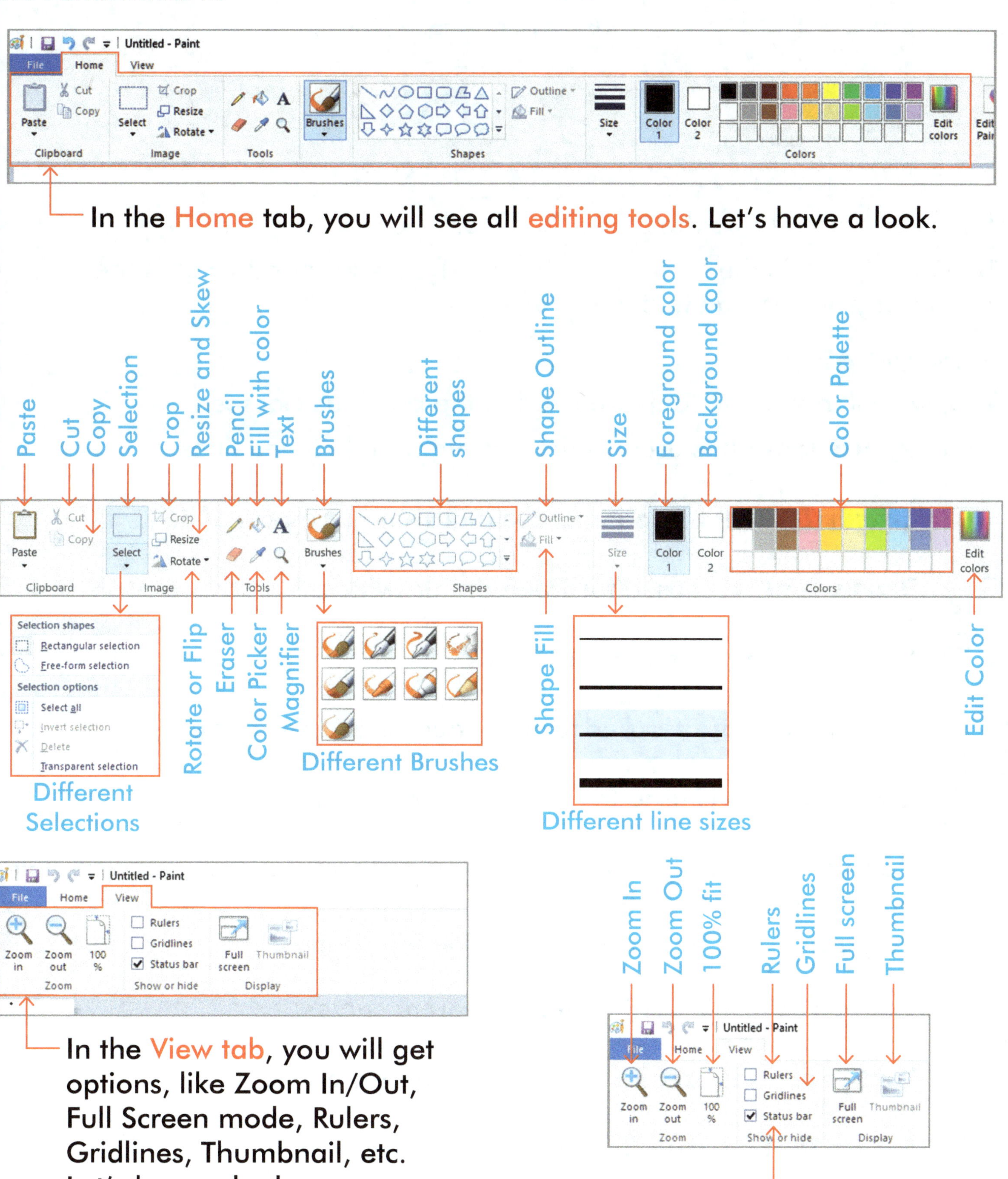



In the Home tab, you will see all editing tools. Let's have a look.

In the View tab, you will get options, like Zoom In/Out, Full Screen mode, Rulers, Gridlines, Thumbnail, etc. Let's have a look.

**Color Palette**: Color palette is also present in the Home tab. You can select the colour you want to work with it.



The Color 1 box shows the active colors or foreground color.

The Color 2 box is the background color. The background color is the default color of any new image that you create.

## Tools in Paint

Now, we will revise the tools we used in the previous classes.

 **Pencil Tool** : It is used to draw straight and curved lines.

 **Eraser Tool** : It is used to erase a drawing or a part of it.

 **Brush Tool** : It is used for freehand drawings.

 **Line Tool** : It is used to draw lines.

 **Rectangle Tool** : It is used to draw squares and rectangles.

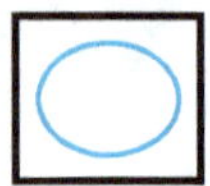 **Circle Tool** : It is used to draw circles or ovals.

 **Rounded Rectangle Tool** : It is used to draw squares and rectangles but with rounded corners.

 **Polygon Tool** : It is used to draw joining shapes.

 **Curve Tool** : It is used to draw different curves.

 **Text Tool** : It is used to write text on your drawing area.

 **Select Tool** : It is used to select the drawing.

# RESIZE AN IMAGE

By using the Resize option, you can change the size of the image by making it narrower, wider, shorter or taller.

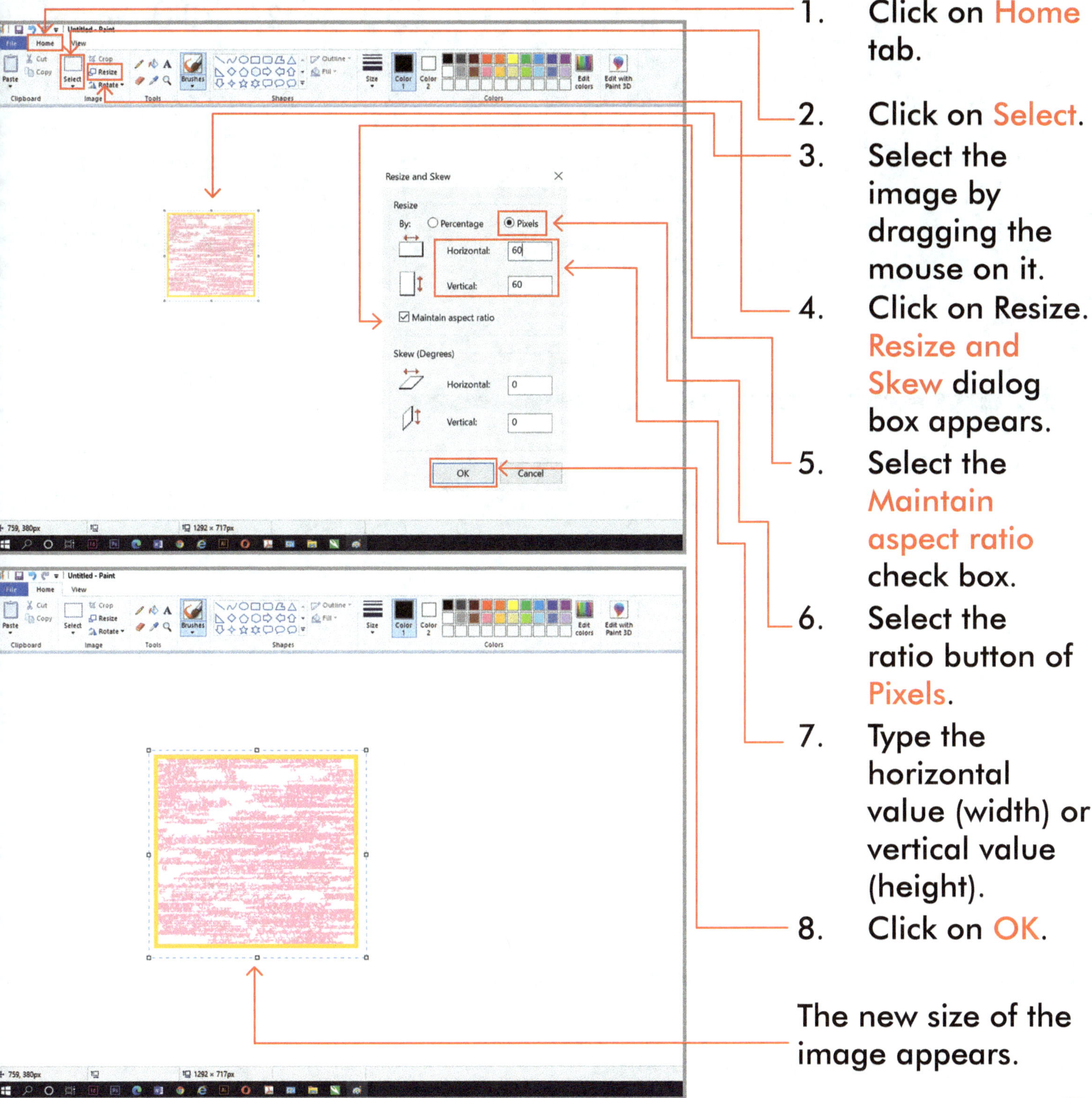

1. Click on Home tab.
2. Click on Select.
3. Select the image by dragging the mouse on it.
4. Click on Resize. Resize and Skew dialog box appears.
5. Select the Maintain aspect ratio check box.
6. Select the ratio button of Pixels.
7. Type the horizontal value (width) or vertical value (height).
8. Click on OK.

The new size of the image appears.

# SKEW AN IMAGE

Skew option is also used to resize the image but through it the image gets stretched from the one end while the other end remains fixed.

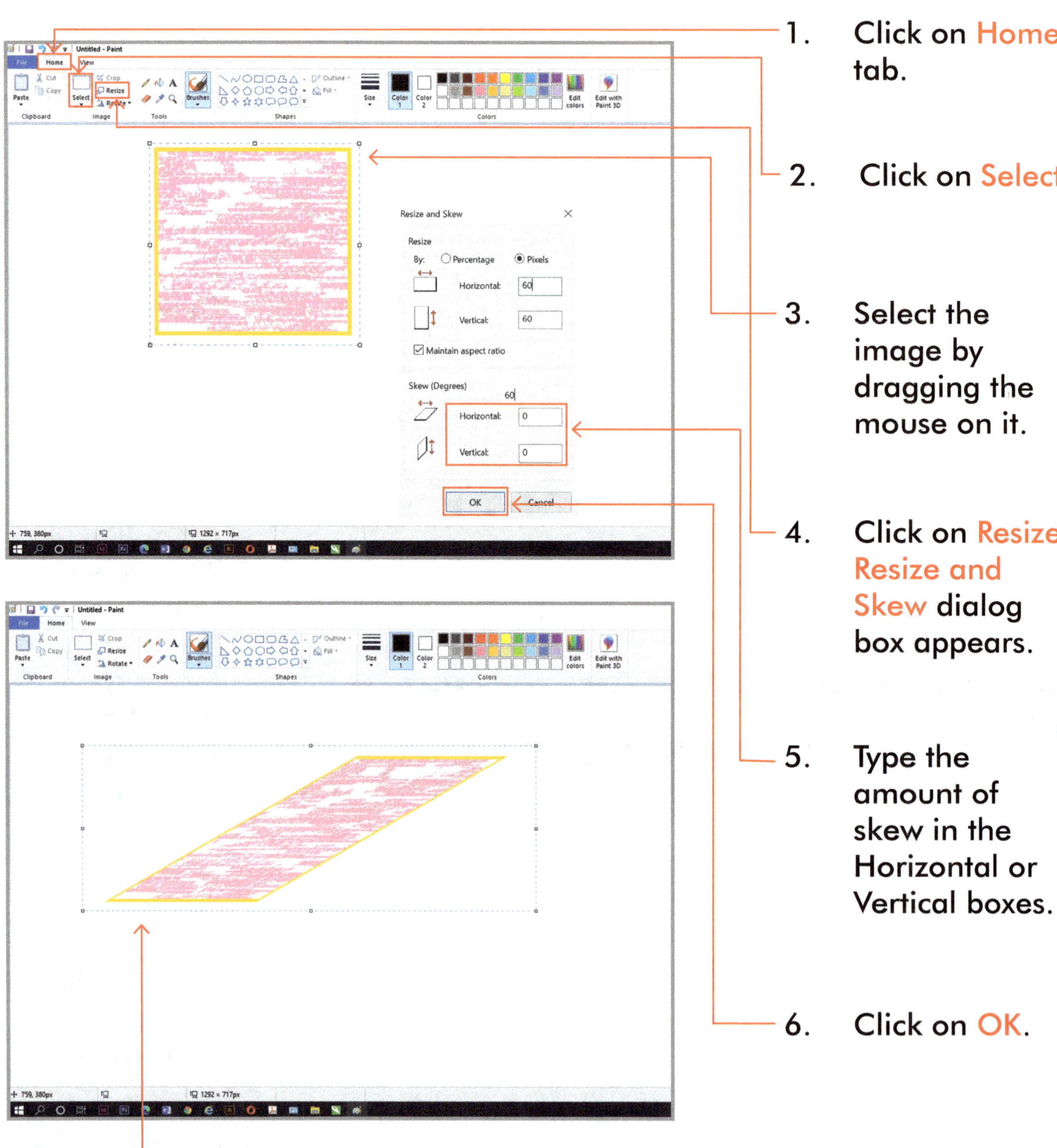



1. Click on **Home** tab.

2. Click on **Select.**

3. Select the image by dragging the mouse on it.

4. Click on **Resize. Resize and Skew** dialog box appears.

5. Type the amount of skew in the Horizontal or Vertical boxes.

6. Click on **OK.**

The skew of the image appears.

# 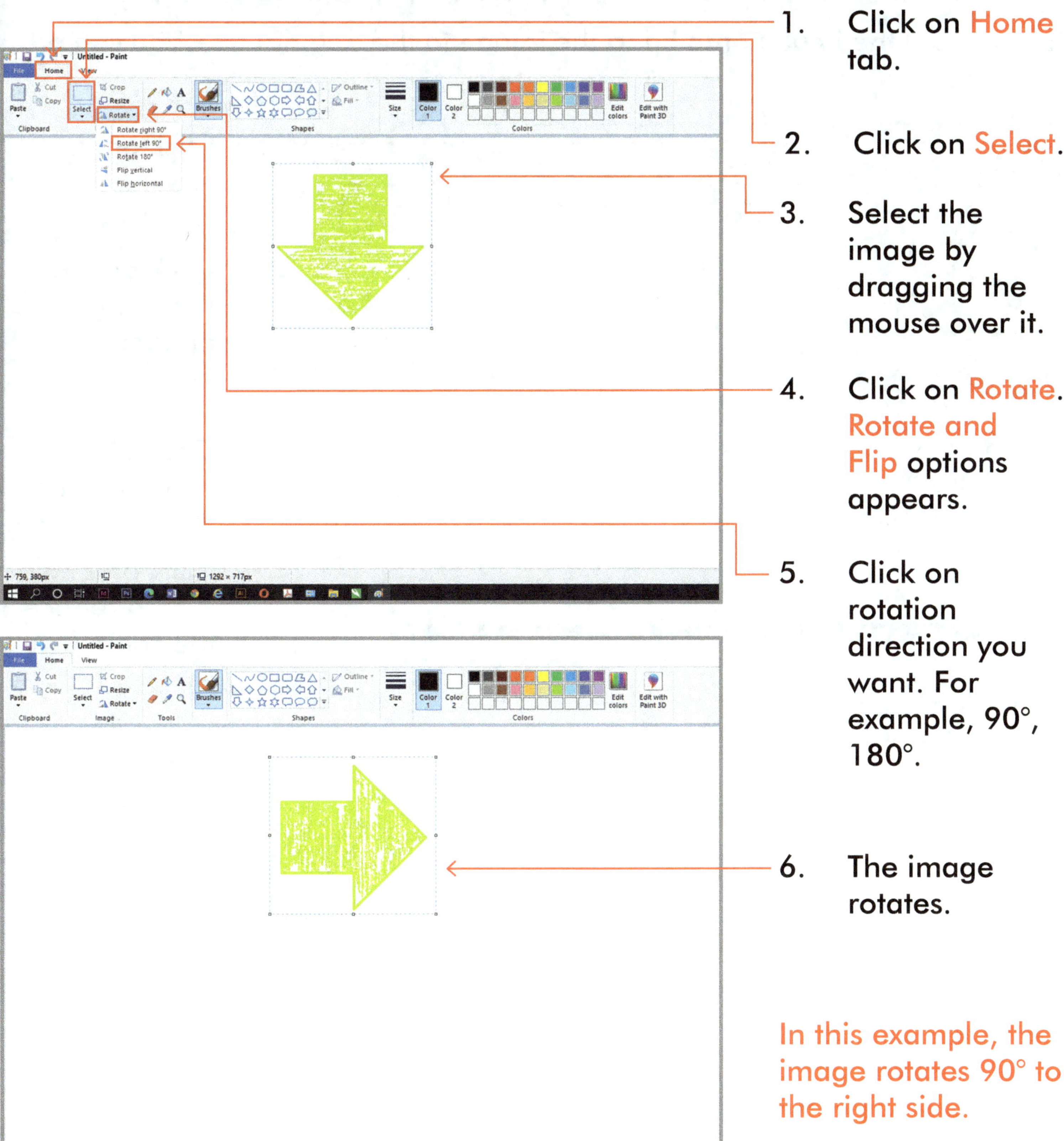

## FLIP AND ROTATE

By using **Flip command**, you can create a **mirror image** of the picture either horizontally or vertically. By using **Rotate command**, you can change the **position** of the image at different **angles**.

1. Click on **Home** tab.

2. Click on **Select**.

3. Select the image by dragging the mouse over it.

4. Click on **Rotate**. **Rotate and Flip** options appears.

5. Click on rotation direction you want. For example, 90°, 180°.

6. The image rotates.

In this example, the image rotates 90° to the right side.

# ZOOM IN AND ZOOM OUT

To get the bigger and smaller view of the image, you can use Zoom In and Zoom Out tool. It is also called magnifying tool.

To zoom in the image, you can also press Ctrl + PgUp.

To zoom out the image or to bring the image to the original size, you can press Ctrl + PgDn.

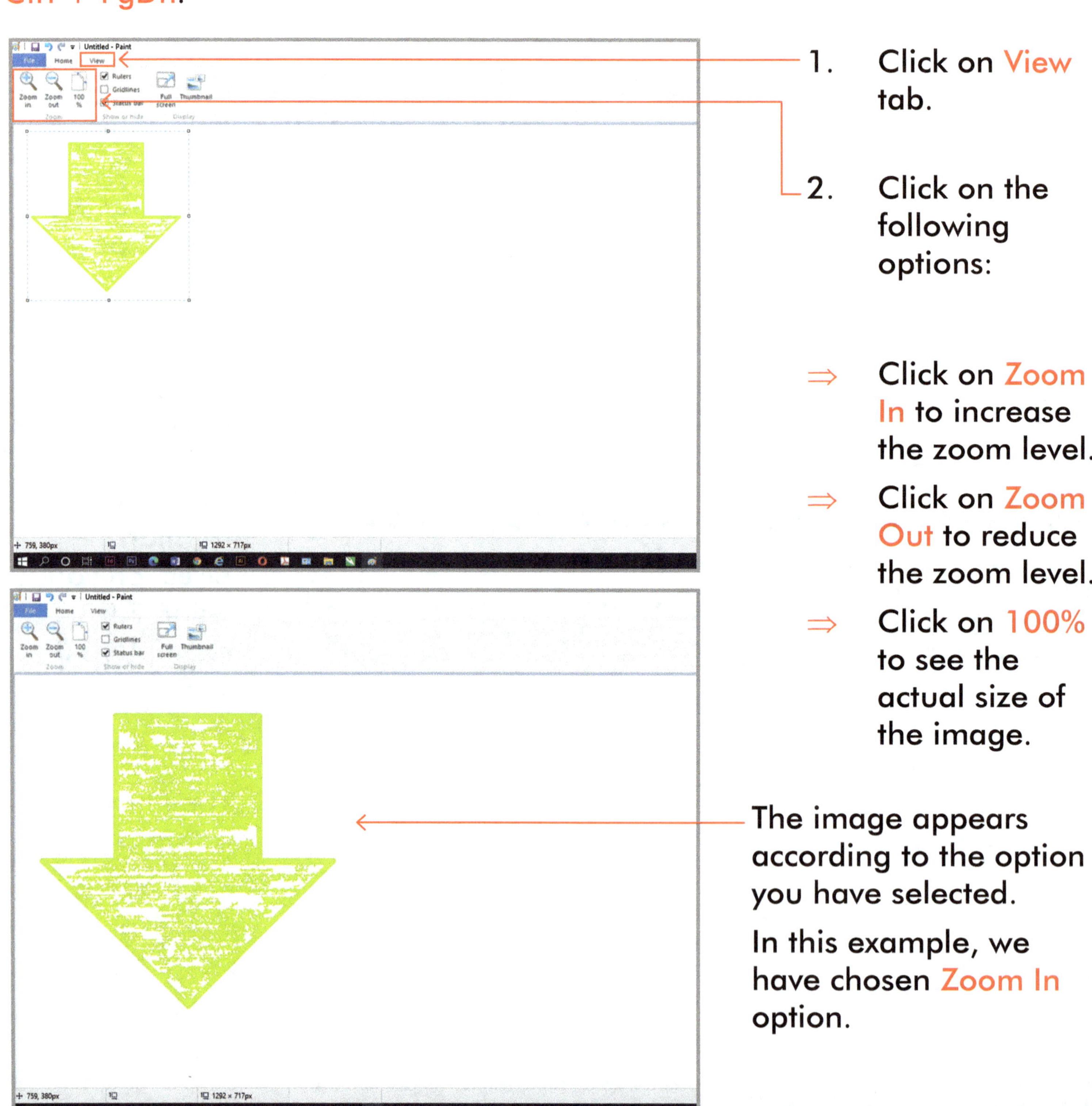

1. Click on View tab.

2. Click on the following options:

   ⇒ Click on Zoom In to increase the zoom level.

   ⇒ Click on Zoom Out to reduce the zoom level.

   ⇒ Click on 100% to see the actual size of the image.

The image appears according to the option you have selected.

In this example, we have chosen Zoom In option.

# CROP IMAGE

You can use the Crop tool to clear the unwanted image from the drawing. After cropping, only the selected part of image is visible.

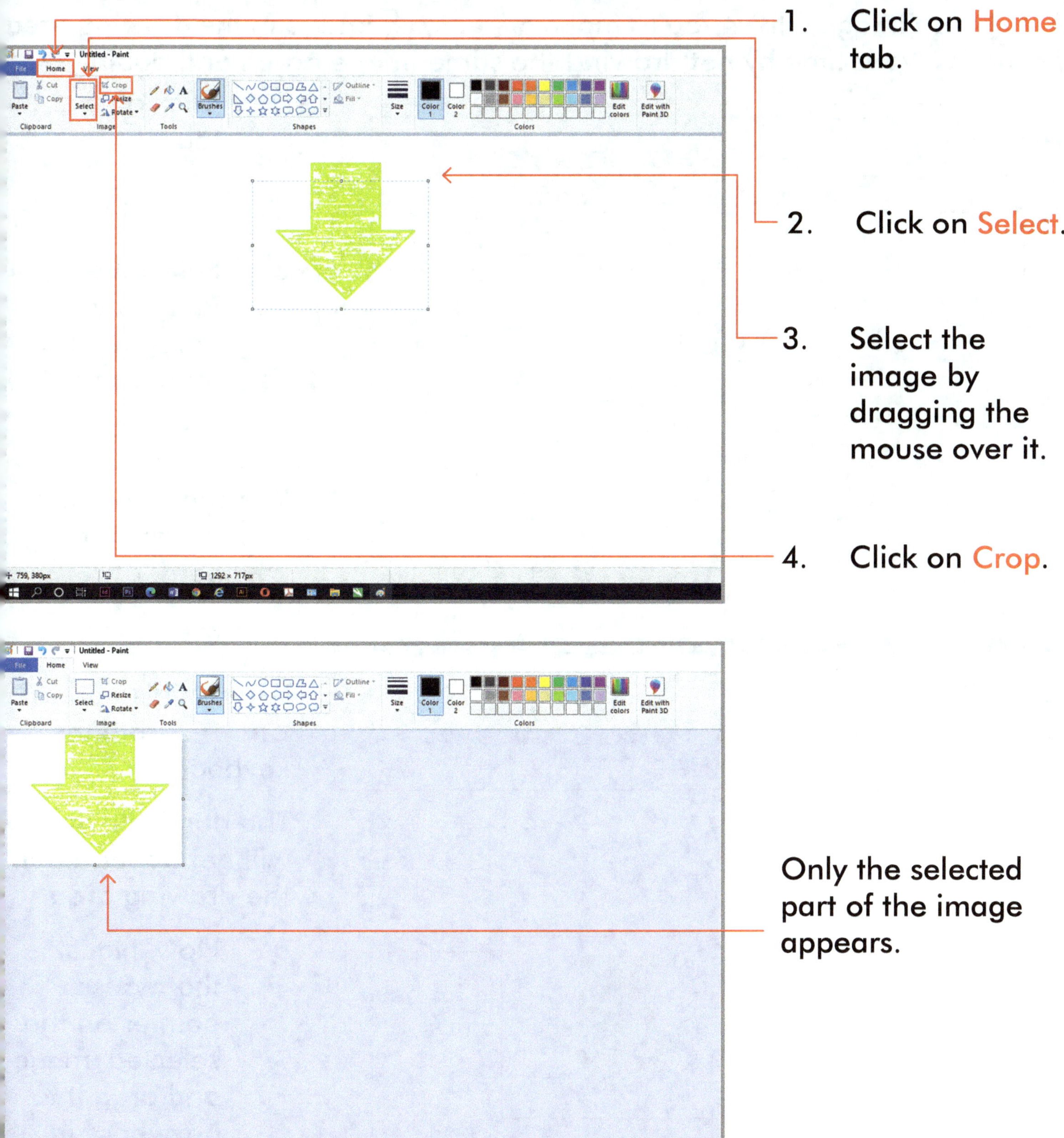

1.  Click on Home tab.

2.  Click on Select.

3.  Select the image by dragging the mouse over it.

4.  Click on Crop.

Only the selected part of the image appears.

# COPY AND PASTE

You can copy the image from one place and paste it at another place through Copy and Paste command.

Copying an image allows you to make a duplicate image in the drawing area. It can save your time by not drawing the same image again and again.

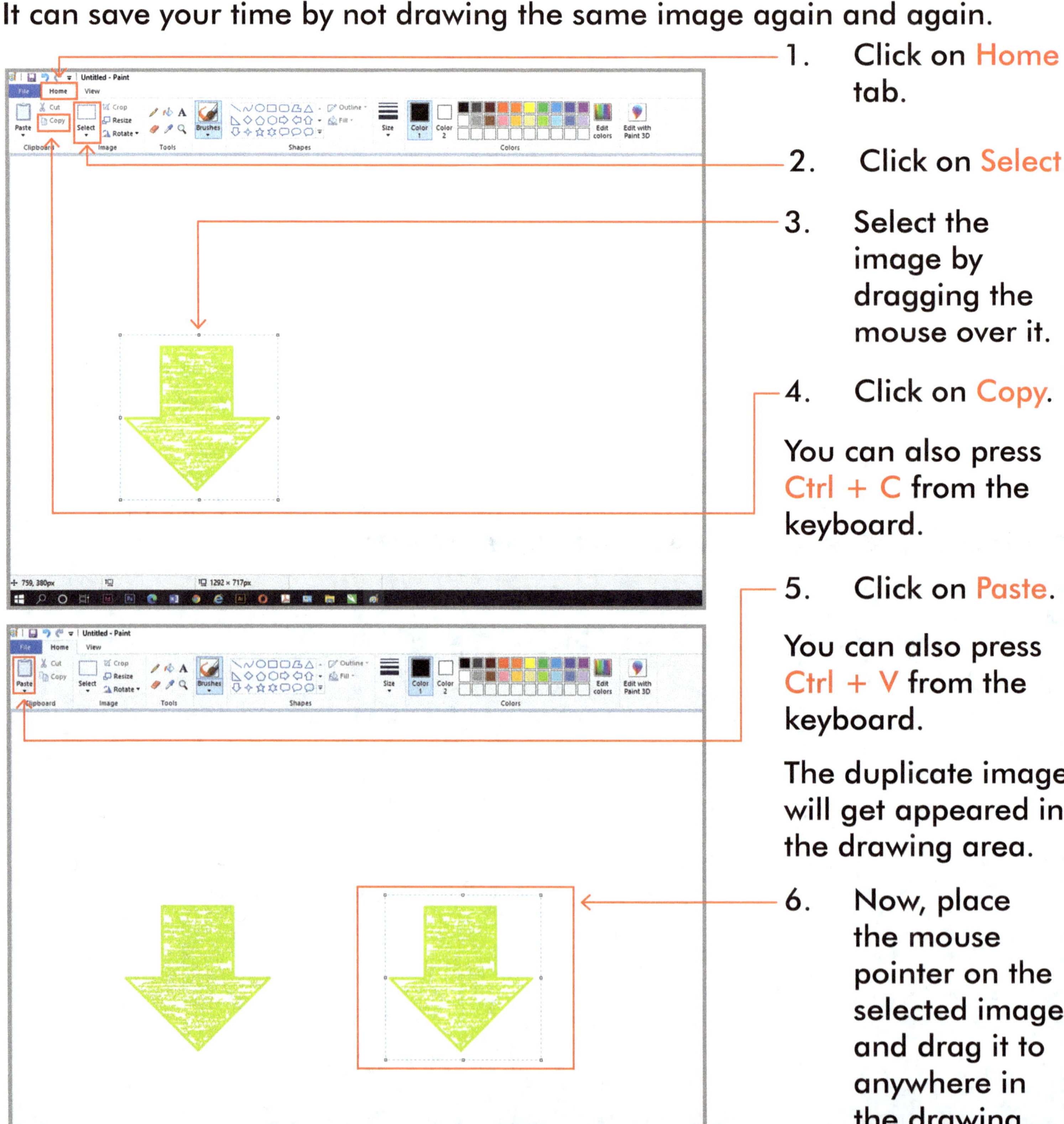

1. Click on Home tab.

2. Click on Select.

3. Select the image by dragging the mouse over it.

4. Click on Copy.

   You can also press Ctrl + C from the keyboard.

5. Click on Paste.

   You can also press Ctrl + V from the keyboard.

   The duplicate image will get appeared in the drawing area.

6. Now, place the mouse pointer on the selected image and drag it to anywhere in the drawing area.

# CUT AND PASTE

Cut and Paste commands are used to cut the image from its original place and paste it on another place within your drawing area.

Cutting an image will make the image disappear from the drawing area.

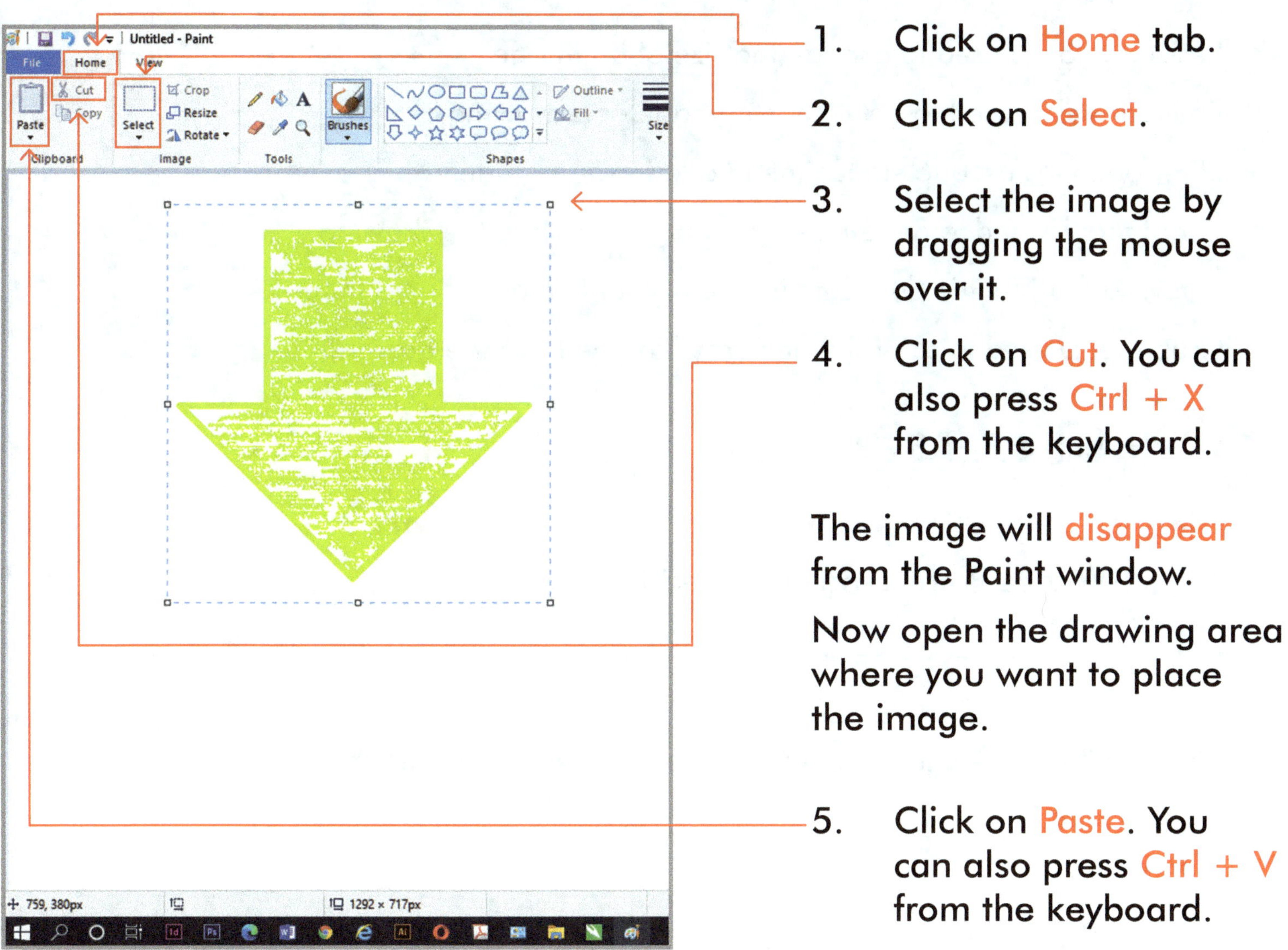

1. Click on Home tab.

2. Click on Select.

3. Select the image by dragging the mouse over it.

4. Click on Cut. You can also press Ctrl + X from the keyboard.

The image will disappear from the Paint window.

Now open the drawing area where you want to place the image.

5. Click on Paste. You can also press Ctrl + V from the keyboard.

# SAVE YOUR IMAGE

To save the image into the memory of the computer, follow the steps:

1. Click on Paint Button. Paint menu will appear.

2. Click on Save.

   The Save As dialog box appears.

3. Type the name for the image in File name text box.

4. Click on Save to save your image.

## LET'S HAVE A LOOK

- Paint is a program used to draw and colour different shapes and images.
- Quick Access Toolbar is the small toolbar that contains the buttons, like Save, Undo and Redo.
- Resize option is used to change the size of an image.
- Flip features is used to get a mirror image of a drawing.
- Skew option is used to stretch the image from one side.
- Zoom tool is used to get a closer and bigger look of the drawing.
- Copy/Paste gives the duplicate image of a drawing.
- Crop tool is used to clear the unwanted image from the drawing.

## BRAIN TEASER

**1.  Write the answers to the following questions:**

a.  What is Paint program used for?

b.  What are the uses of Home tab and View tab?

c.  What is the use of Crop tool?

d.  What is the use of Zoom tool?

e. Name the buttons present on Quick Access Toolbar.

_______________________________________________

_______________________________________________

f. Differentiate between:

i. Flip and Rotate

_______________________________________________

_______________________________________________

_______________________________________________

ii. Skew and Resize

_______________________________________________

_______________________________________________

_______________________________________________

## 2. Write 'T' for true and 'F' for false in the boxes:

a. Paint is a program used to draw and colour images. ☐

b. Crop tool is used to make a duplicate of an image. ☐

c. Skew option is used to stretch the image from one side. ☐

d. Quick Access Toolbar is located at the right corner of the window. ☐

e. Color palette is present in View tab. ☐

f. There are three tabs in Paint Program. ☐

## 3. Multiple Choice Questions

### Tick (✓) the correct answer:

a. The tool used to draw a rounded rectangle

i. ☐   ii. ☐   iii. ☐

b. The tab that contains the editing tools

i. Home tab ☐   ii. View tab ☐   iii. Quick tab ☐

c. The option to clear the unwanted image

    i. Skew ☐    ii. Resize ☐    iii. Crop ☐

d. Shortcut key to copy

    i. Ctrl + C ☐    ii. Ctrl + V ☐    iii. Ctrl + X ☐

e. The option used to copy the drawing from one place to anothe place

    i. Cut/Paste ☐    ii. Copy/Paste ☐    iii. Crop Image ☐

f. Keys pressed to Zoom In the image

    i. Ctrl + PgDn ☐    ii. Ctrl + Z ☐    iii. Ctrl + PgUp ☐

**4. Match each action to its keyboard shortcut:**

| Action | Keyboard shortcut |
| --- | --- |
| a. Creating a new drawing | Ctrl+S |
| b. Saving a new drawing | Ctrl+X |
| c. Cuting a part of a drawing | Ctrl+C |
| d. Copying a part of a drawing | Ctrl+V |
| e. Paste a part of a drawing | Ctrl+N |

**5. Fill in the blanks:**

a. _______________ is the program in which you can draw and colou different images.

b. _______________ tool is used to see a closer and bigger look o your drawing.

c. _______________ option is used to create the mirror image of the drawing.

d. _______________ option is used to stretch the image from one end

e. _______________ and _______________ are two tabs in the Pain program.

Paste · Cut · Copy · Clipboard · Select · Crop · Resize · Rotate · Image · A · Brushes · Tools · Outline · Fill · Shapes · Size · Color 1 · Color 2 · Colors · Edit colors

Selection shapes
- Rectangular selection
- Free-form selection

Selection options
- Select all
- Invert selection
- Delete
- Transparent selection

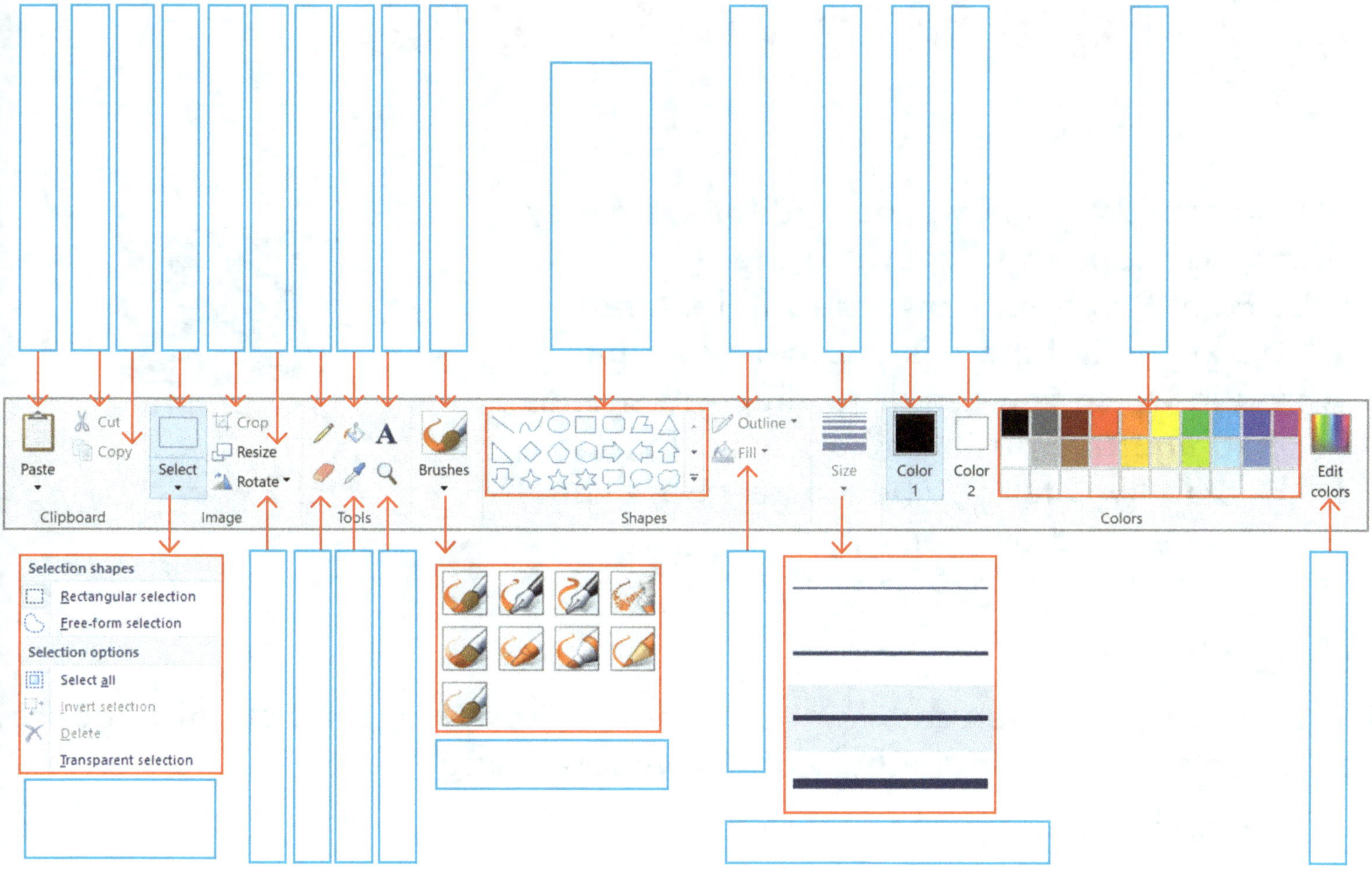

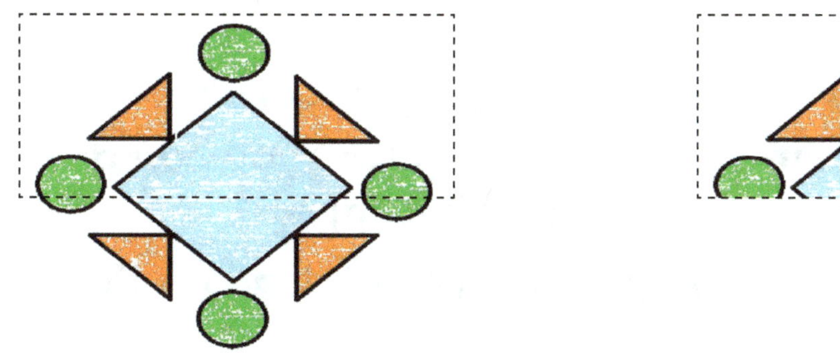

## LAB ACTIVITY

**Visit your computer lab, open Paint and try to draw the following:**

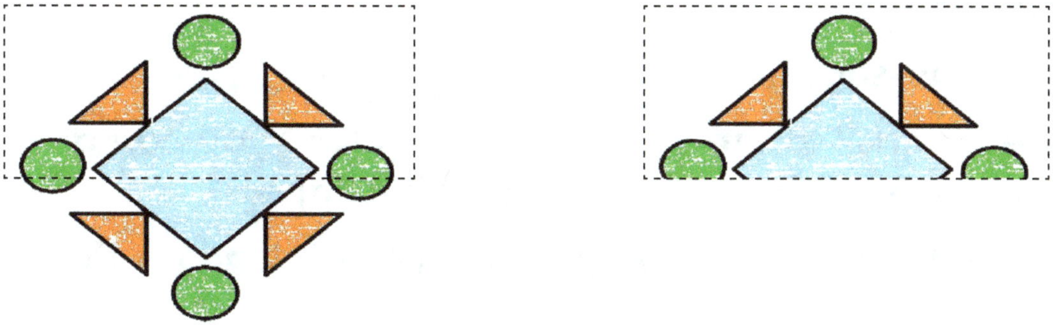

- Select the part marked, copy it and paste to the right side.
- Flip and rotate the image.
- Resize the image by making it taller.
- Save the image.

# 6 Starting with LOGO

Hello friends! Till now, you had lots of fun by drawing shapes and figures using a mouse in the Paint Program. Now, you will be amazed to know that there is another program through which you can draw different shapes and figures by using a keyboard. In this chapter, I will tell you how a keyboard can draw. Let's start.

## LOGO

Children, as you have used Paint program to draw with the help of a mouse, you can also draw with the help of a keyboard using LOGO.

LOGO stands for Language of Graphics Oriented.

LOGO is a programming language in which you give commands through a keyboard to draw any shapes and figures.

**You can use LOGO to do various works like –**

⇒ Draw figures and shapes

⇒ Do calculations

⇒ Displaying messages

Just as we use a pencil to draw on paper, in LOGO you can draw with Turtle. Turtle is like a pen of LOGO. It is triangular in shape.

Let us know how to use LOGO language while working on the computer.

**Do you know** ?

LOGO was developed by a group of experts headed by Mr Seymour Papert, of MIT, USA, in year 1967.

## STARTING LOGO

1. Click on the Start button.
2. Click on the All Programs.
3. Click on MSW LOGO.

After following the above steps, you will get the LOGO screen as:

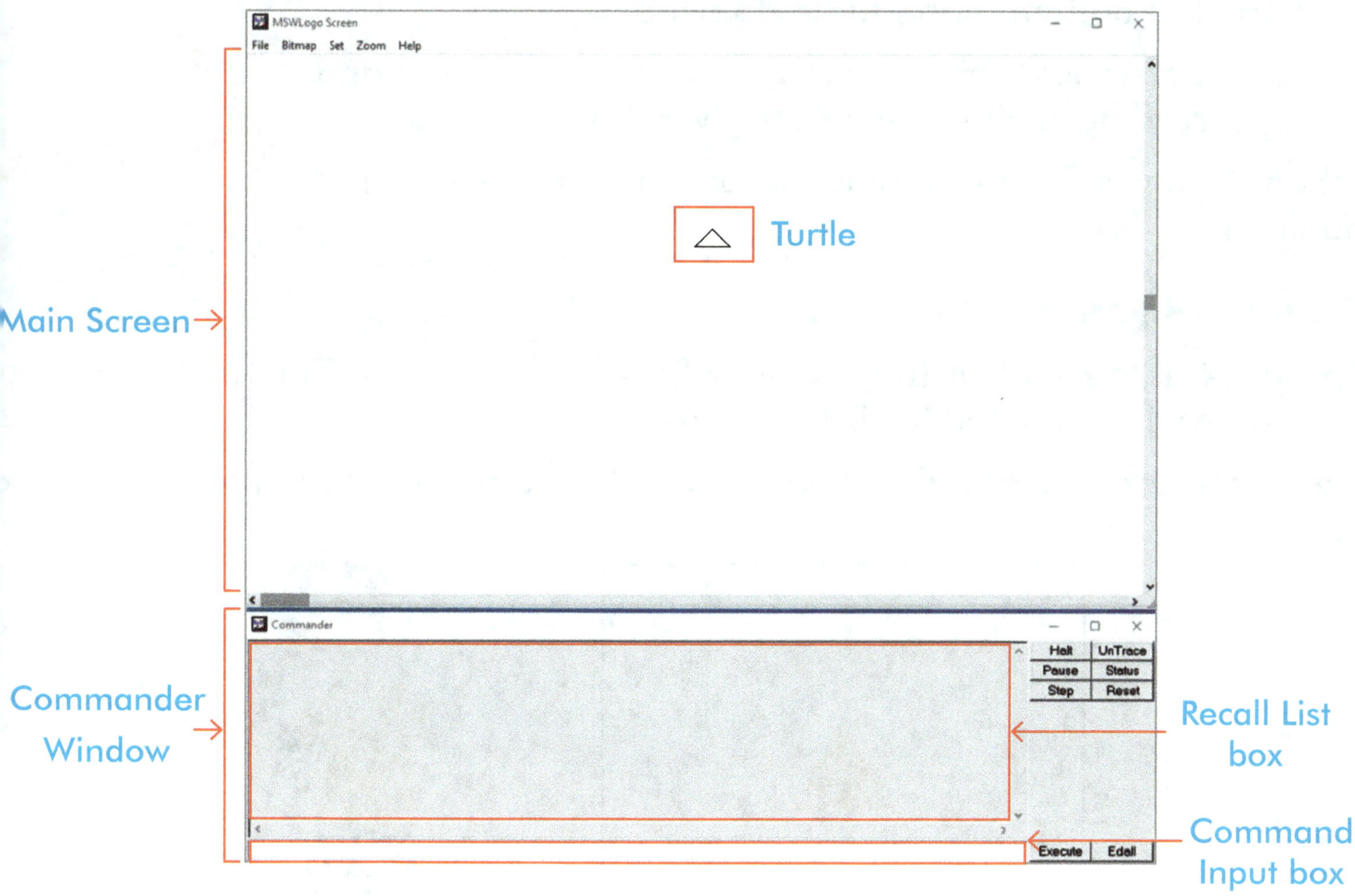


LOGO screen is mainly divided into two parts:

**Main Screen**: It is the drawing area which contains a turtle. The turtle obeys the commands given by us and performs actions.

**Commander Window**: It is the area where the user can type the commands of LOGO. These commands are called Primitives.

**Command Input box**: It is the area where all the LOGO commands are written and executed by pressing the Enter key or by clicking on the Execute button.

**Recall List box**: It is the area that keeps the track of all the commands that are executed.

## LOGO'S TURTLE

The small triangle present at the centre of the LOGO screen is called turtle. Turtle works like a pen in LOGO.

Turtle has two parts:

⇒ The pointed top of the turtle is called head.

⇒ The flat bottom of the turtle is called its tail.

Turtle understands only LOGO commands. It moves and draws according to the commands given by you.

When it moves from one place to another, it draws a line behind it.

## Turtle's Home

The turtle is present in the middle of the Main Screen. This is the starting position of the turtle, which is known as Home.

The blank area of a Main screen where the turtle moves is the field of the turtle.

## LOGO PROMPT

LOGO Prompt is the question mark (?) that appears in the Commander window.

## EXIT LOGO

You can exit LOGO by typing 'Bye' in the Command Input box and press the Enter key from the keyboard.

## LET'S HAVE A LOOK

- LOGO is a program used to draw shapes by typing commands using the keyboard.
- The full form of LOGO is Language of Graphics Oriented.
- The LOGO screen is divided into two parts – Main Screen and Commander Window.
- Main screen is the graphic area where shapes are drawn.
- Commander window is the area where commands are written.
- Turtle is a small triangle in the centre of the Graphic screen.
- The question mark (?) is the LOGO Prompt after which the commands are written.

## BRAIN TEASER

**1. Write the answers to the following questions:**

a. What is the use of LOGO?

b. What is the difference between Paint program and LOGO?

c. Name the two parts into which the LOGO screen is divided

d. What is the use of Command Input box?

e. Who developed LOGO and when?

f. What is turtle?

**2. Answer in one word or sentence:**

   a.   What is the full form of LOGO?

   b.   What is the shape of a turtle?

   c.   Name the parts of a turtle.

   d.   Where is the home of the turtle?

   e.   What is LOGO Prompt?

**3. Fill in the blanks:**

   a.   LOGO is a ________________ language.

   b.   LOGO was developed by ________________.

   c.   The turtle is of ________________ shape.

   d.   ________________ area contains the turtle.

   e.   The symbol ________________ is a LOGO Prompt.

**4. Match the following:**

   a.   LOGO was developed by              Head and tail

   b.   Two parts of LOGO screen           Sir Seymour Papert

   c.   Turtle                             Main screen

   d.   Parts of the turtle                Home of the turtle

   e.   The area where a figure is drawn   Triangle

   f.   Centre of the main screen          Main screen and
                                           commander window

**5.** **Write 'T' for true and 'F' for false in the boxes:**

a. LOGO was developed by Bill Gates. ☐

b. The shape of the turtle is square. ☐

c. The LOGO screen is divided into two parts. ☐

d. The LOGO prompt is '?'. ☐

**6.** **Multiple Choice Questions**

**Tick (✓) the correct answer:**

a. A programming language

   i. MS-Word ☐    ii. MS-Paint ☐    iii. LOGO ☐

b. The small triangle in the centre of screen

   i. Turtle ☐    ii. Commander ☐    iii. Reset Button ☐

c. The commands are written in

   i. Main Screen ☐    ii. Turtle ☐

   iii. Commander window ☐

d. A command used to exit from LOGO

   i. Exit ☐    ii. Out ☐    iii. Bye ☐

**7.** **Label the following window:**

**1.** **Write the names of the following tools:**

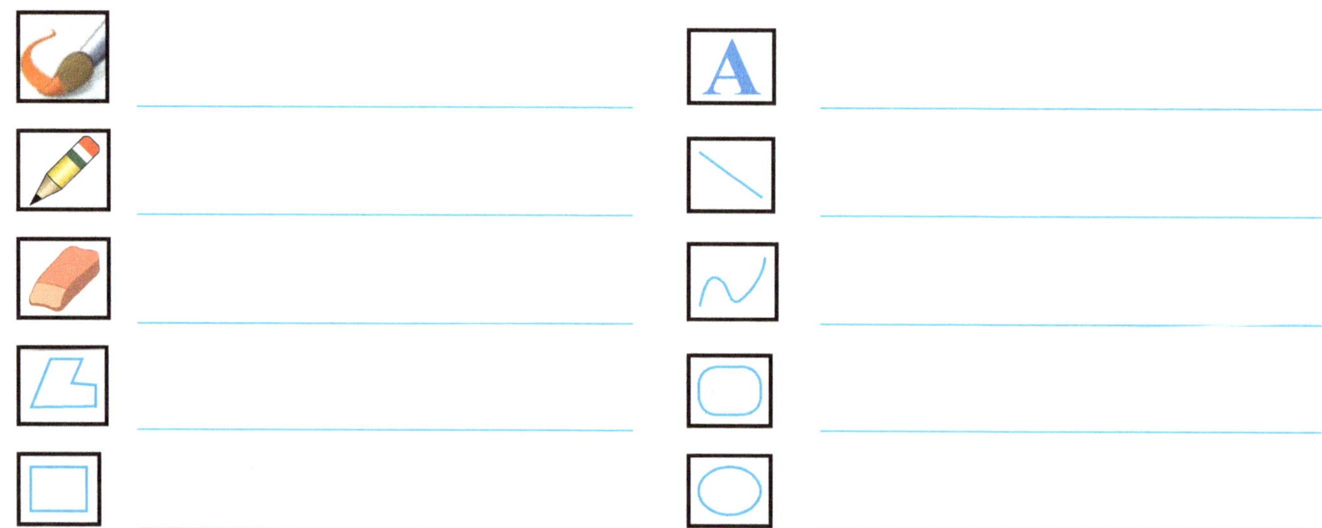

**2.** **Find out the hidden turtle in the grid:**

(Hint: The word **TURTLE** appears 8 times.)

| T | U | R | T | L | E | T | L | E |
| T | U | T | U | R | T | L | E | T |
| U | T | U | R | T | L | R | U | R |
| R | U | R | T | U | R | T | L | E |
| T | R | T | L | R | T | U | R | T |
| L | T | L | E | T | T | U | R | T |
| E | L | E | U | L | T | U | R | T |
| T | E | R | T | E | T | U | R | T |

**3.** **Write the full form of LOGO:**

# 7 Working with LOGO

## LOGO PRIMITIVES

LOGO commands are the instructions that you give to the turtle to draw any shape.

The commands that you give to the turtle are called LOGO Primitives.

Some important primitives and their short forms are given below.

| PRIMITIVES | SHORT FORMS |
|---|---|
| FORWARD | FD |
| BACK | BK |
| RIGHT | RT |
| LEFT | LT |
| HIDETURTLE | HT |
| SHOWTURTLE | ST |
| CLEARSCREEN | CS |

FD (Forward)

LT (Left)

RT (Right)

## MOVING COMMANDS

You can use FD and BK commands to move the turtle.

## FORWARD (FD)

The FORWARD or FD primitive or command is used to move the turtle in forward direction.

**Syntax :**

> FD <space> (number of steps) <Enter>

**FD 50 <Enter>**

It will move the turtle fifty steps forward.

## BACKWARD (BK)

The BACKWARD or BK primitive or command is used to make the turtle move in backward direction.

**Syntax :**

> BK <space> (number of steps) <Enter>

**BK 30 <Enter>**

It will move the turtle thirty steps backward.

## TURNING COMMANDS

RT and LT are the two turning commands used in LOGO.

## RIGHT (RT)

The RIGHT or RT primitive or command is used to turn the turtle to the right side in the clock-wise direction.

**Syntax :**

> RT <space> (number of turns) <Enter>

**RT 90 <Enter>**

It will turn the face of the turtle in the right direction by 90 turns.

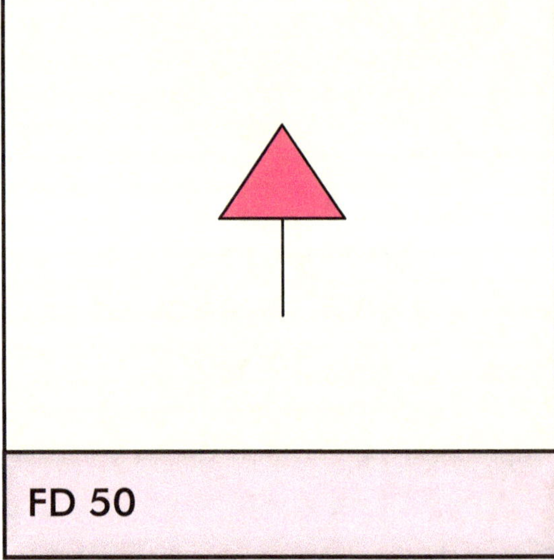


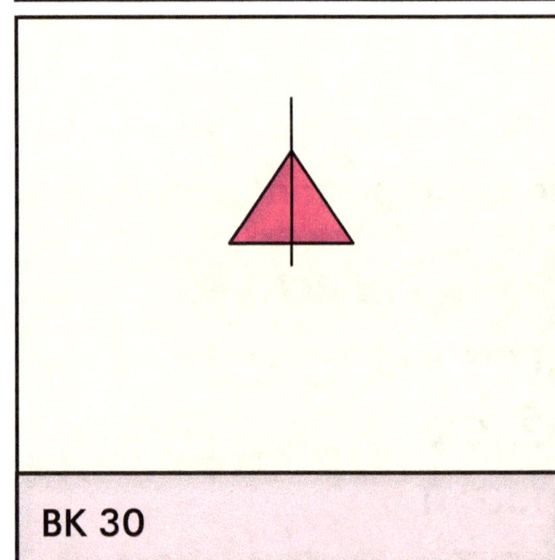


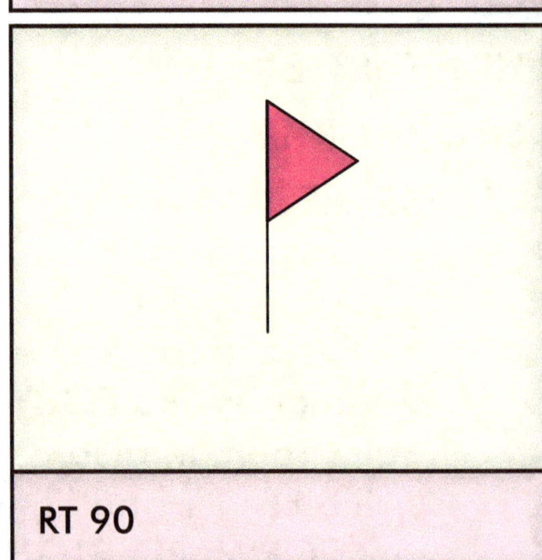

# LEFT (LT)

LEFT or LT command is used to turn the turtle to the left side in the anticlock-wise direction.

Syntax :

```
LT <space> (number of turns) <Enter>
```

**LT 90 <Enter>**

It will turn the face of the turtle in the left direction by 90 turns.

## TURTLE'S PEN COMMANDS

The pen of the turtle can be lifted up or down with the help of the commands.

### PENUP (PU)

PENUP command is used to lift the turtle penup. Let it move without drawing any line on the screen.

Syntax :

```
PU or PENUP <Enter>
```

**PU <Enter>**

**FD 50 <Enter>**

It will move the turtle 50 steps ahead in the forward direction without leaving a trail behind as the PU command is given before FD command.

### PENDOWN (PD)

PENDOWN command will again lift the turtle pen down and start drawing again on the screen.

Syntax :

```
PD or PENDOWN <Enter>
```

**PD <Enter>**

**FD 20 <Enter>**

This command lifts the turtle pendown on the screen. Move forward 20 steps.

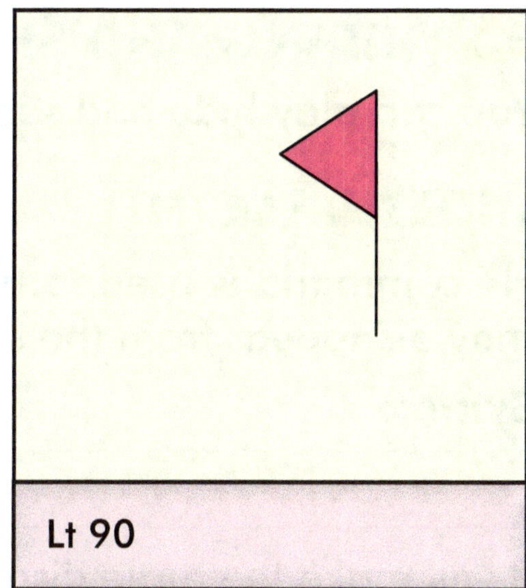


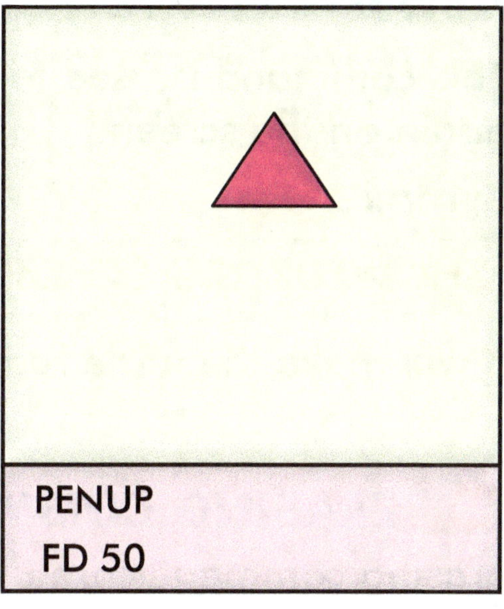


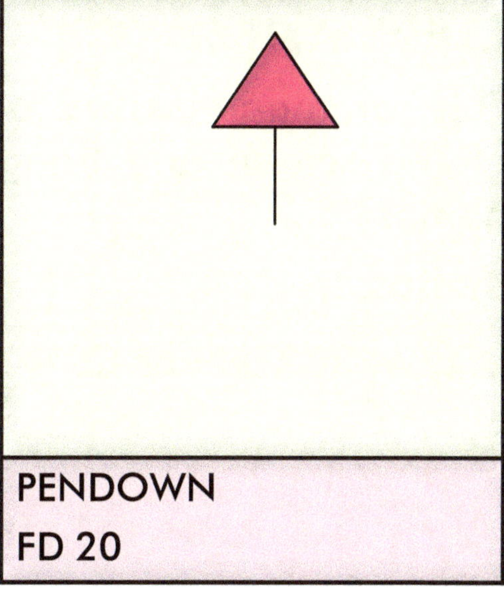

# HIDING AND SHOWING THE TURTLE

You can play hide and seek with the turtle by using commands.

## HIDETURTLE (HT)

HT command is used to hide the turtle so that it may disappear from the screen.

**Syntax :**

| HIDETURTLE or HT <Enter> |

It will make the turtle disappear from the screen.

HIDETURTLE

## SHOWTURTLE (ST)

This command is used to show the hidden turtle again on the screen.

**Syntax :**

| SHOWTURTLE or ST <Enter> |

It will make the turtle reappear on the screen.

SHOWTURTLE

# ERASING COMMANDS

Erasing commands are used to erase or clear the screen.

## CLEARSCREEN (CS)

This command is used to clear the drawing area of the screen and bring back the turtle to its home.

**Syntax :**

| CLEARSCREEN or CS <Enter> |

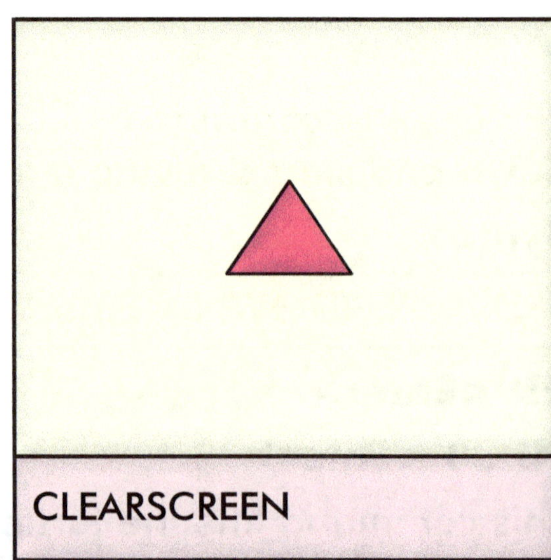

CLEARSCREEN

# CLEARTEXT (CT)

This command is used to clear the text written in command window.

**Syntax** :

> CLEARTEXT or CT <Enter>

It will make the turtle disappear from the screen.

# HOME

HOME command is used to bring the turtle to its home from any position by leaving the line behind.

**Syntax** :

> HOME <Enter>

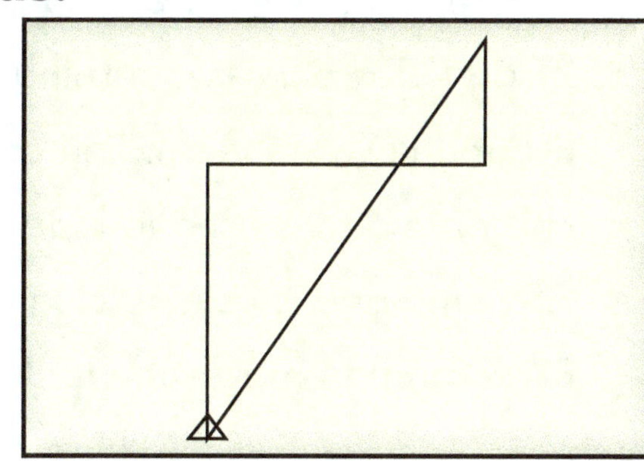


**Example**

**Now, try some examples using the commands:**

FD 100 <Enter>

RT 90 <Enter>

FD 100 <Enter>

LT 90 <Enter>

FD 40 <Enter>

Home <Enter>

Home command lets the turtle leave a trail behind and come back to its home. It is pointed in the upward direction.

**Draw a figure using PU and PD primitives.**

FD 50 <Enter>

PU <Enter>

RT 90 <Enter>

FD 20 <Enter>

RT 90 <Enter>

PD <Enter>

FD 50 <Enter>

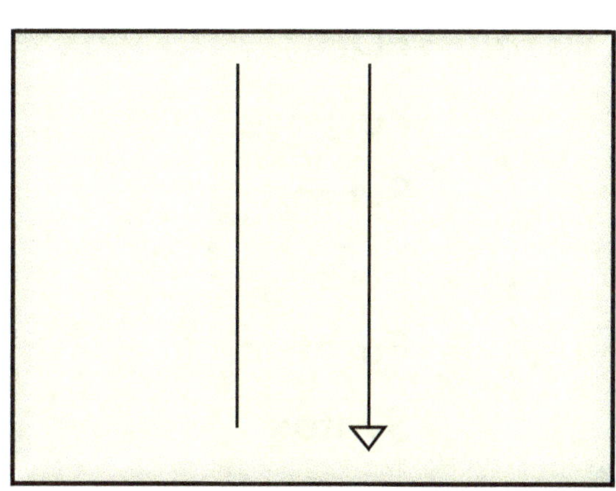

**Try one more figure.**

FD 100 <Enter>

RT 90 <Enter>

FD 50 <Enter>

RT 90 <Enter>

FD 50 <Enter>

HOME <Enter>

RT <Enter>

FD 50 <Enter>

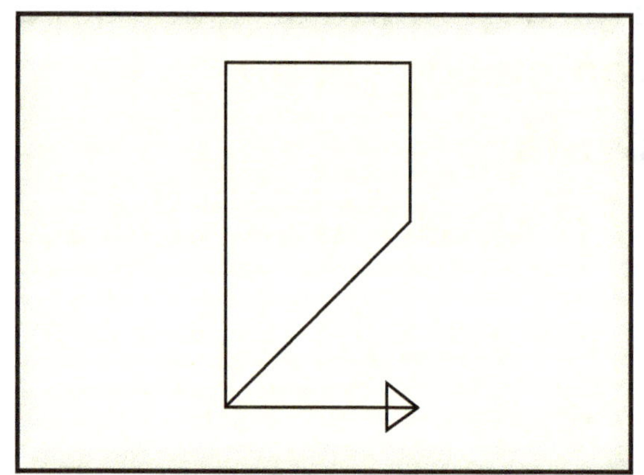

- The instruction given as a command is known as Primitive.
- Different Primitives are used to draw shapes in LOGO.
- RT and LT are the two turning commands that turn the face of the turtle.
- PU and PD are the two Pen commands.
- HT command is used to hide the turtle from the screen.
- CS command is used to clear the Graphic Screen.
- BK command moves the turtle in the backward direction.

1.  **Give the purpose and syntax of each of the following commands:**

    a.  FD

        Purpose ___________________________________________

        Syntax ___________________________________________

    b.  BK

        Purpose ___________________________________________

        Syntax ___________________________________________

c.  RT

Purpose ______________________________________________

Syntax ______________________________________________

d.  PU

Purpose ______________________________________________

Syntax ______________________________________________

e.  CS

Purpose ______________________________________________

Syntax ______________________________________________

## 2. Give the full form of each of the following:

a.  FD ______________________________________________

b.  BK ______________________________________________

c.  RT ______________________________________________

d.  LT ______________________________________________

e.  HT ______________________________________________

f.  ST ______________________________________________

g.  CS ______________________________________________

h.  LOGO ____________________________________________

## 3. Fill in the blanks:

a.  LOGO commands are also called ______________ .

b.  ______________ and ______________ are the turtle pen commands.

c.  ______________ command will move the turtle in the right direction.

d.  ______________ command will move the turtle by 20 steps forward.

e.  The ______________ is used to bring the turtle back to its home.

## 4. Multiple Choice Questions

**Tick (✓) the correct answer:**

a. The command used to move turtle in the forward direction
   i. FD ☐      ii. RT ☐      iii. BK ☐

b. The command used to turn the face of the turtle towards the left
   i. RT ☐      ii. HT ☐      iii. LT ☐

c. The command used to lift the turtle Pendown
   i. PD ☐      ii. PU ☐      iii. UP ☐

d. Which is used to bring the turtle to the centre of the drawing area?
   i. Draw ☐      ii. Home ☐      iii. CT ☐

e. The moving primitives
   i. CS & CT ☐      ii. PU & PD ☐      iii. FD & BK ☐

## LAB ACTIVITY

1. **Write LOGO commands to draw the following figures:**

**2.** **Type the following commands in LOGO and draw the figure:**

CS <Enter>

FD 50 <Enter>

RT 90 <Enter>

FD 10 <Enter>

RT 90 <Enter>

FD 20 <Enter>

LT 90 <Enter>

FD 20 <Enter>

LT 90 <Enter>

FD 20 <Enter>

RT 90 <Enter>

FD 10 <Enter>

RT 90 <Enter>

FD 50 <Enter>

RT 90 <Enter>

FD 10 <Enter>

RT 90 <Enter>

FD 20 <Enter>

LT 90 <Enter>

FD 20 <Enter>

LT 90 <Enter>

FD 20 <Enter>

HOME

# 8 Introduction to MS-Word

## MS-WORD

MS-Word is a word processing program developed by Microsoft. It has many advanced features that help us to create beautiful documents by using the keyboard.

In MS-Word, you can change the font and colour of the text. It can also check your spelling mistakes. You can add borders, shading, tables, graphics and pictures in documents.

## STARTING MS-WORD 2016

To start Ms-Word, follow the given steps:

1. Click on Start Button.

2. Click on All Programs.

3. Click on Microsoft Office.

4. Click on Microsoft Word 2016.

The Microsoft Word will appear.

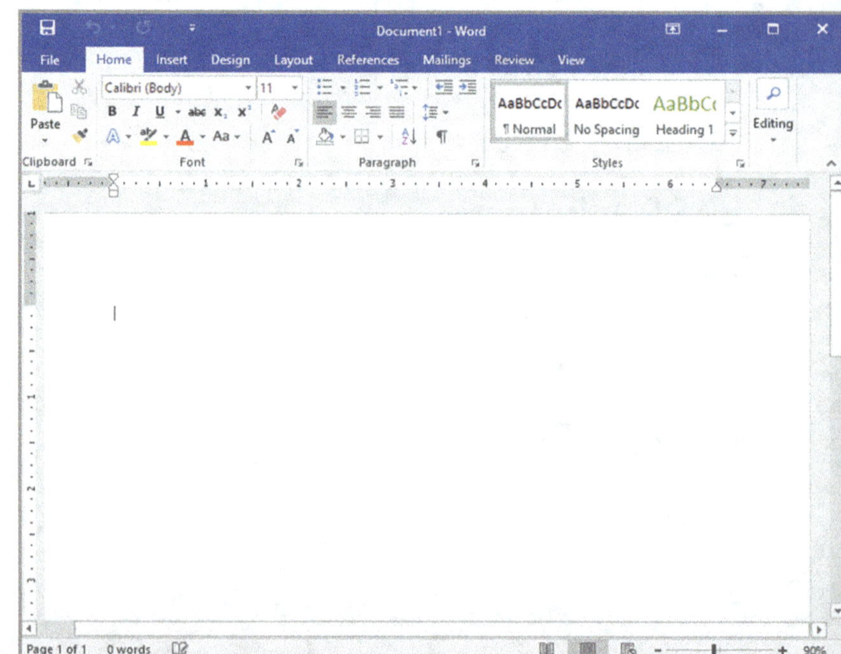

MS-Word Window ⟶

# MS-WORD WINDOW

After opening MS-Word, an empty document titled Document 1 appears on your screen.

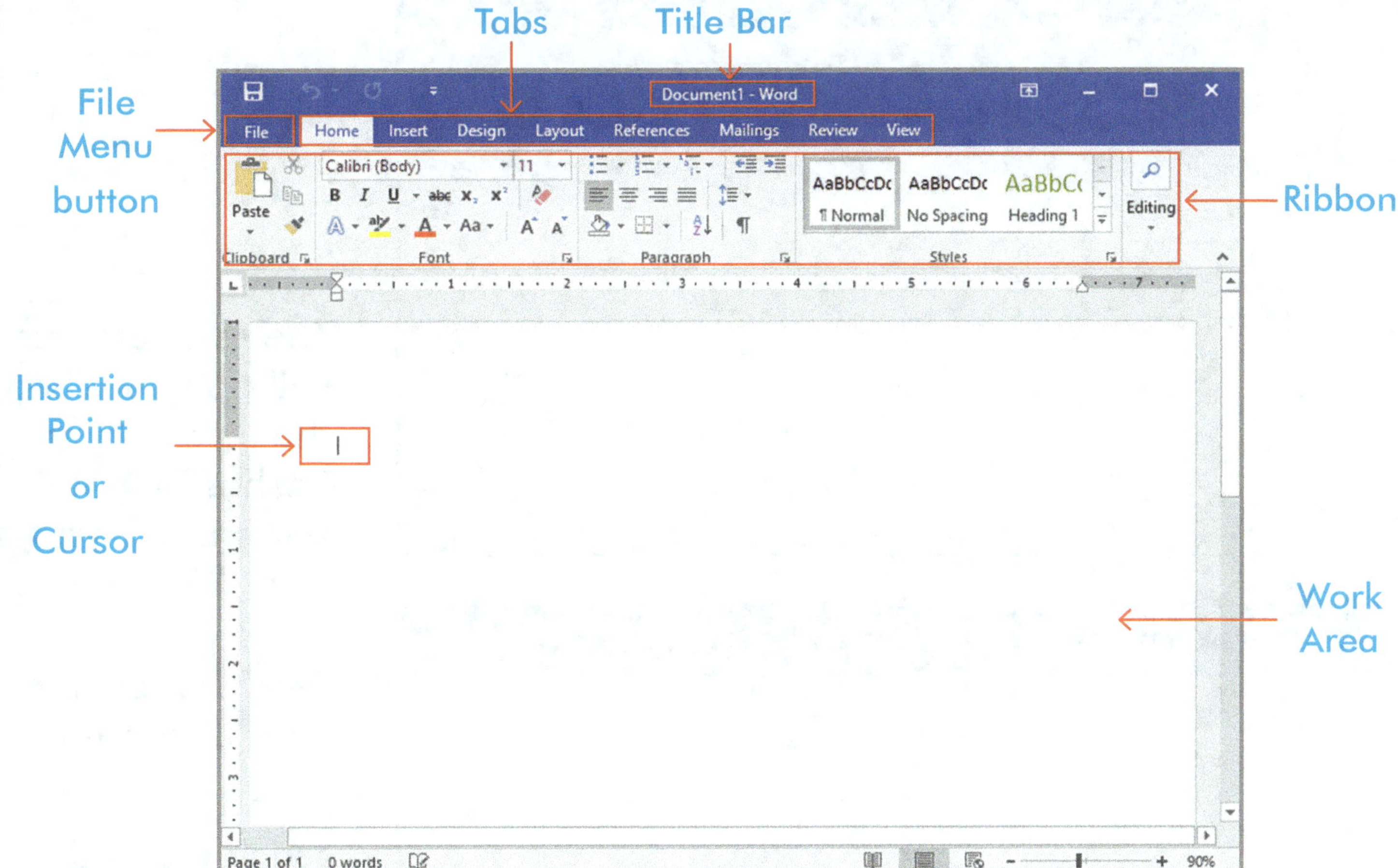


**Title Bar**: It is the topmost bar that shows the name of the displayed document and program.

**File Menu button**: Click to display a drop-down menu, which displays the commands, such as New and Open.

**Ribbon**: Displays the groups of related commands in tabs. Each tab offers shortcut buttons to common tasks.

**Tabs**: Each tab provides a set of tools related to an overall task you are likely to perform in a specific application.

**Insertion Point**: Insertion point is a vertical flashing line on the screen that shows the current position when you type.

**Work Area**: Main area in the document where you type the text of your document.

# ENTERING TEXT

You can enter the text with the help of the keyboard.

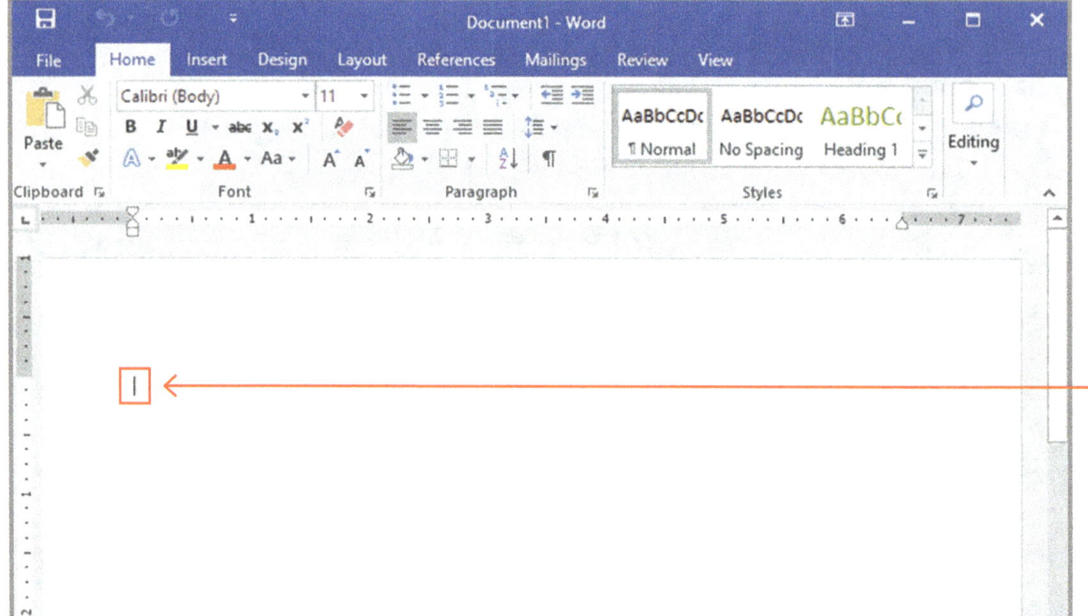

The text you type will appear where the insertion point flashes on your screen.

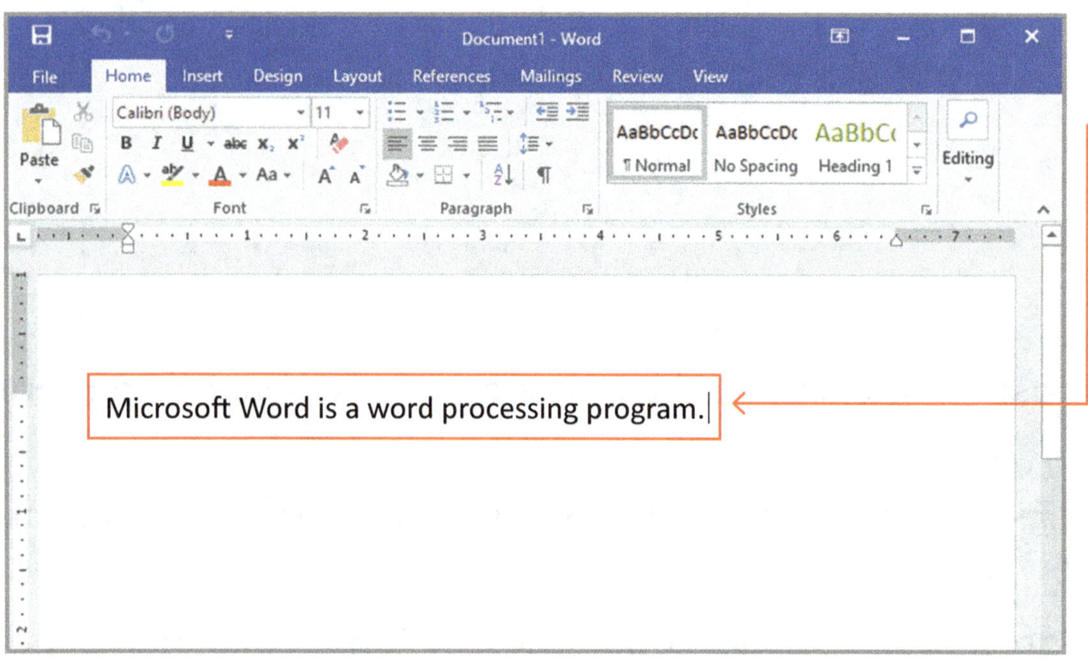


Type the text for your document.

When you reach the end of a line, Word automatically sends the text to the next line. You only press the Enter key when you want to start a new paragraph.

# SAVING A DOCUMENT

The document must be saved into the memory of the computer for its future use.

In MS-Word, your document will be saved in the form of files. These files will have .DOC extension.

Once you have saved your work, you can use it in future as well.

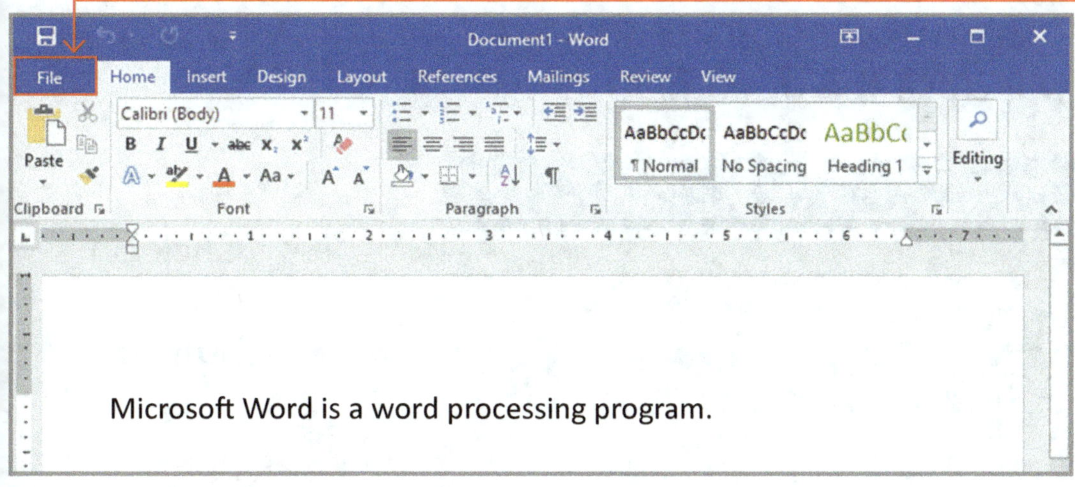

Microsoft Word is a word processing program.

1. Click on **File menu** button.

   **Backstage view** will appear.

**Do you know** ?

*Backstage view shows the options, like Save, Open, Print, New, etc.*

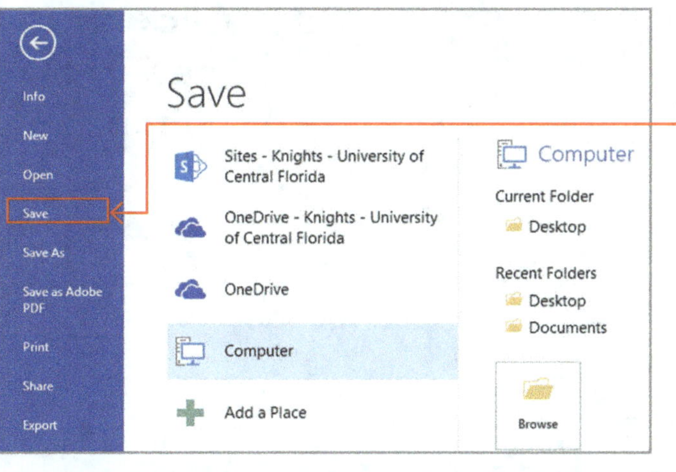

2. Click on **save** button in Backstage view.

   The **Save As** dialog box appears.

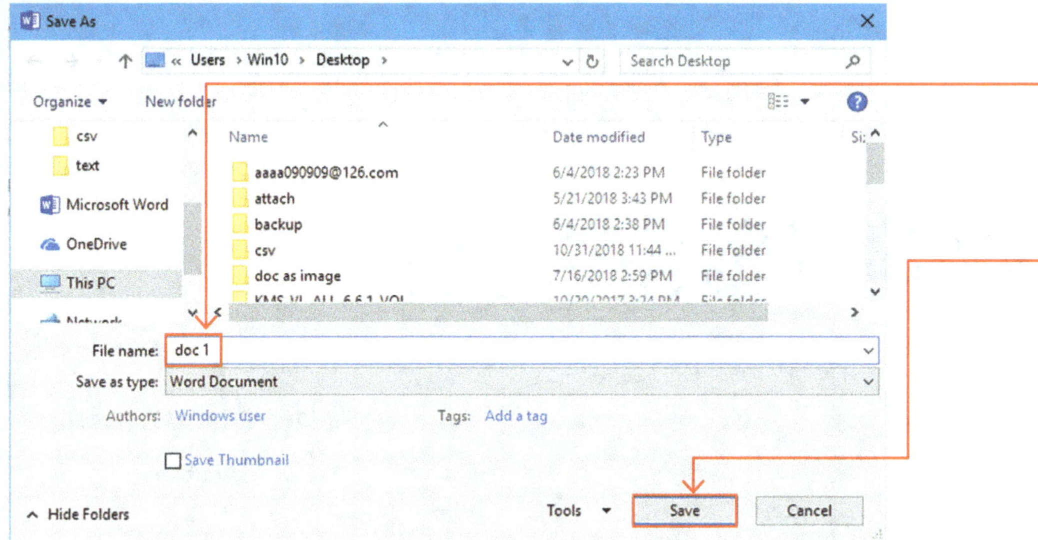

3. Type a name for the **file** in this area.

4. Click on **Save** button.

   The Word saves the file and the new file name appears on the title bar.

**Note**

*The shortcut keys for saving a document are Ctrl + S.*

# CLOSING A DOCUMENT

**Closing the document will close the open file.**

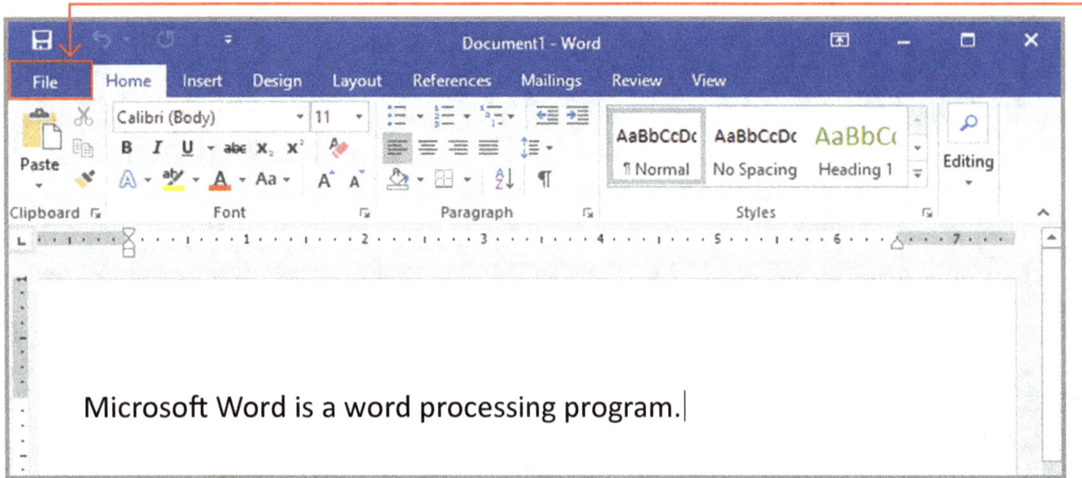

1. Click on **File menu** button.

   **Backstage view** will appear.

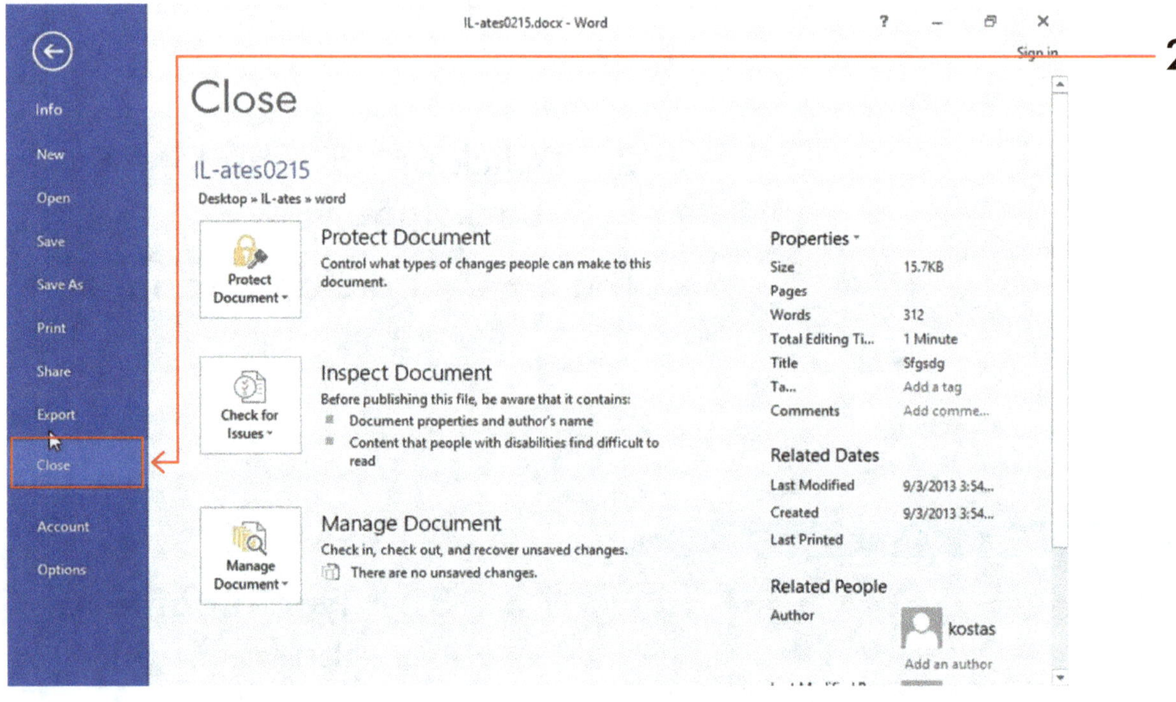

2. Click on the **Close** button.

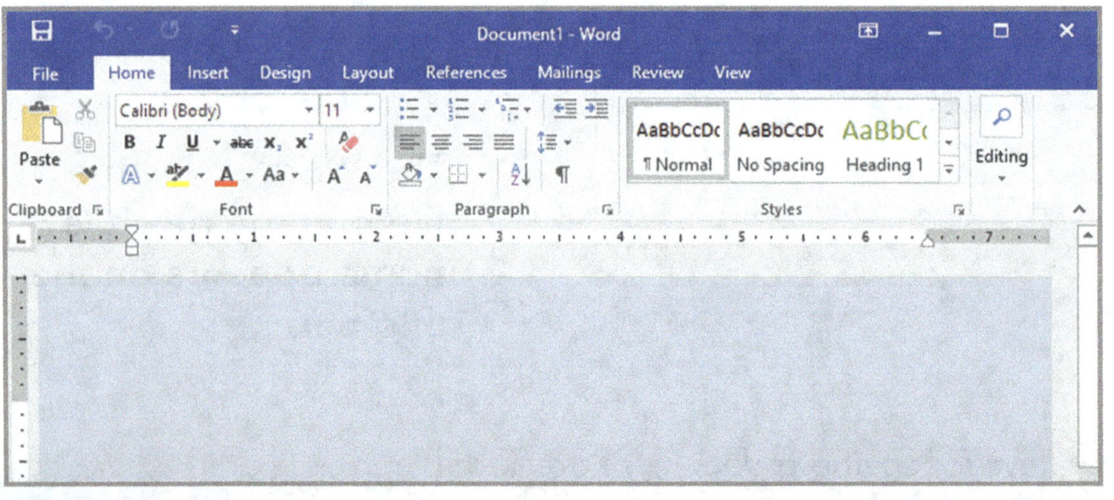

The document file closes.

# OPENING A SAVED DOCUMENT

You can open the already saved document to review or edit. To open the already saved document, the steps are:

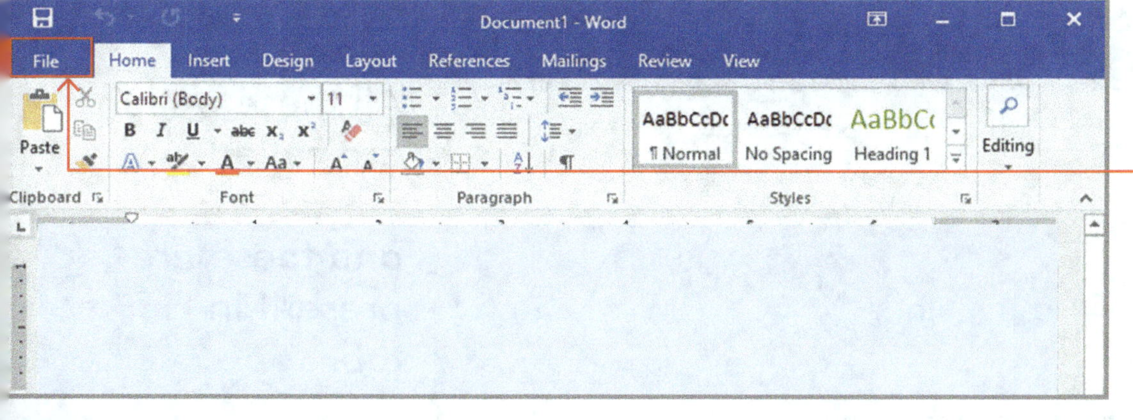

1. Click on **File menu** button.

   **Backstage view** will appear.

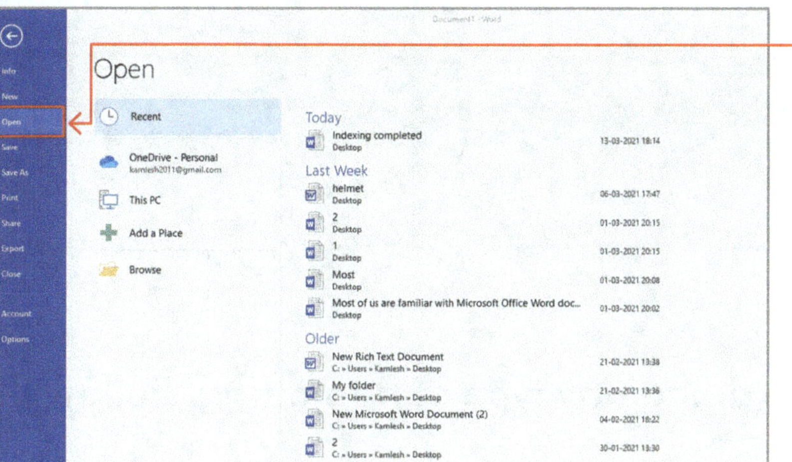

2. Click on **Open** button.

   The **Open** dialog box appears.

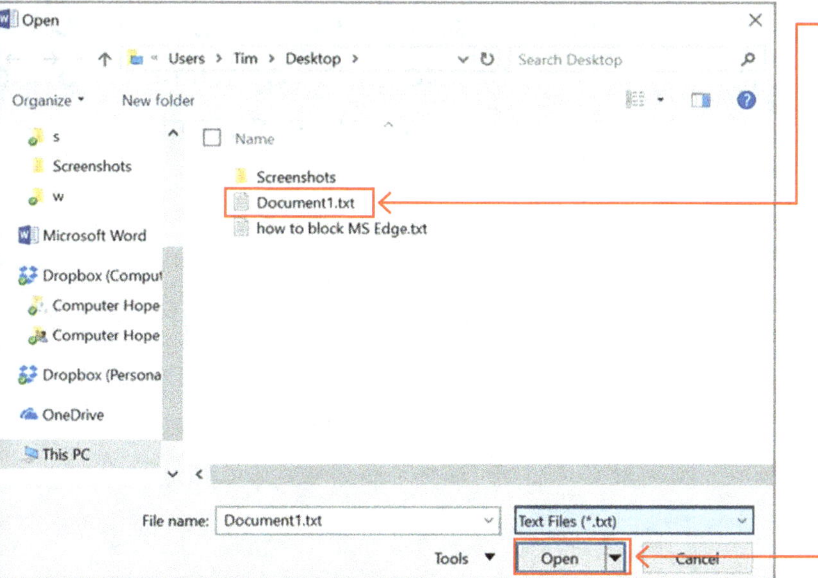

3. Click on the **name of the file** that you want to open.

4. Click on **Open** button.

   The file opens in the program window.

**Note**

*The shortcut keys for opening a document are Ctrl + O.*

# FORMATTING TEXT

In MS-Word, you can make your text more beautiful, colourful and impressive.

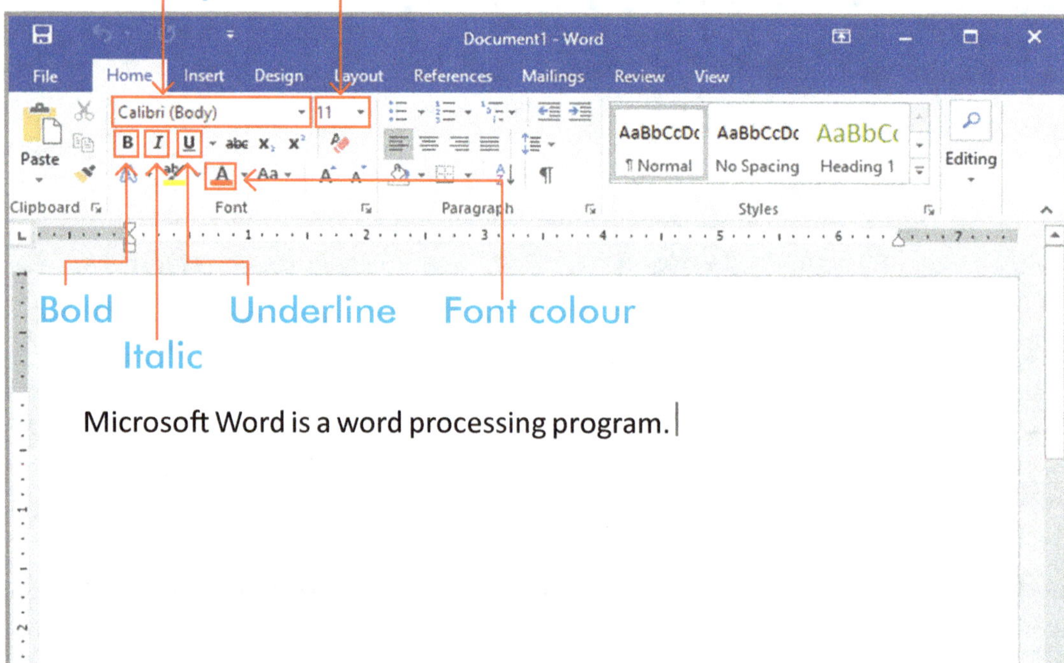


All these options are called Formatting options and these are present in Home tab.

# SELECTING TEXT

You have to select the text first before doing any type of formatting. Follow the steps to select the sentence below:

Microsoft Word is a word processing program.

1. Place the mouse pointer in the start of the sentence you want to select.

Microsoft Word is a word processing program.

2. Now press the left button, drag till the text is highlighted and release the button.

or

Press Shift + Right arrow key from the keyboard to select the text.

# BOLD, ITALIC AND UNDERLINE TEXT

By using bold, italic or underline feature of MS-Word, you can make your text darker, slanting and underline to make your document interesting.

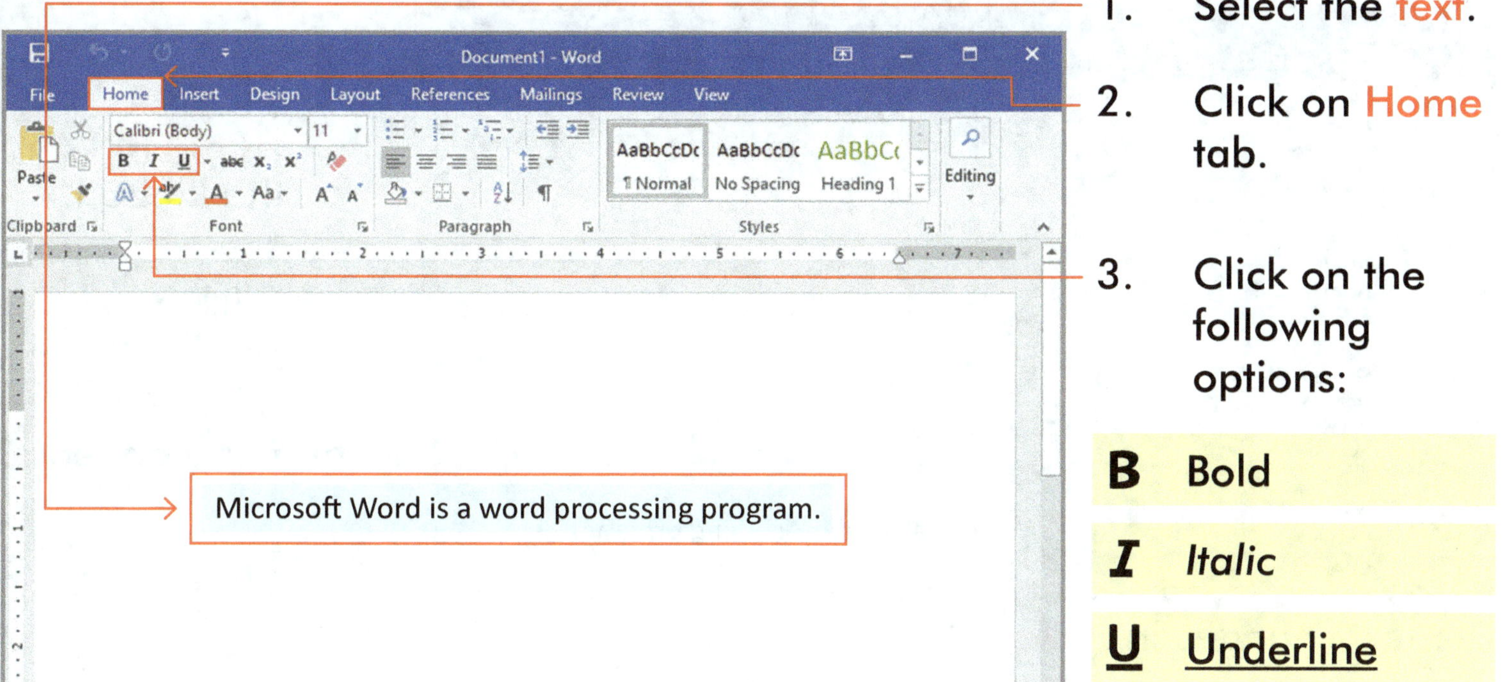


1. Select the text.

2. Click on Home tab.

3. Click on the following options:

**B** Bold

*I* Italic

**U** Underline

The text appears **darker** if you select **Bold** in step **3**.

> **Microsoft Word is a word processing program.**

The text appears **slanting** if you select **Italic** in step **3**.

> *Microsoft Word is a word processing program.*

The text appears **underlined** if you select **Underline** in step **3**.

> <u>Microsoft Word is a word processing program.</u>

**Do you know** ❓

The keyboard shortcut to bold text is Ctrl + B.

**Do you know** ❓

The keyboard shortcut to italic text is Ctrl + I.

**Do you know** ❓

The keyboard shortcut to underline text is Ctrl + U.

To **remove** the Bold, Italic or Underline style, repeat the steps **1** to **3**.

# CHANGE FONT STYLE

This option allows to apply different writing styles by choosing the different fonts.

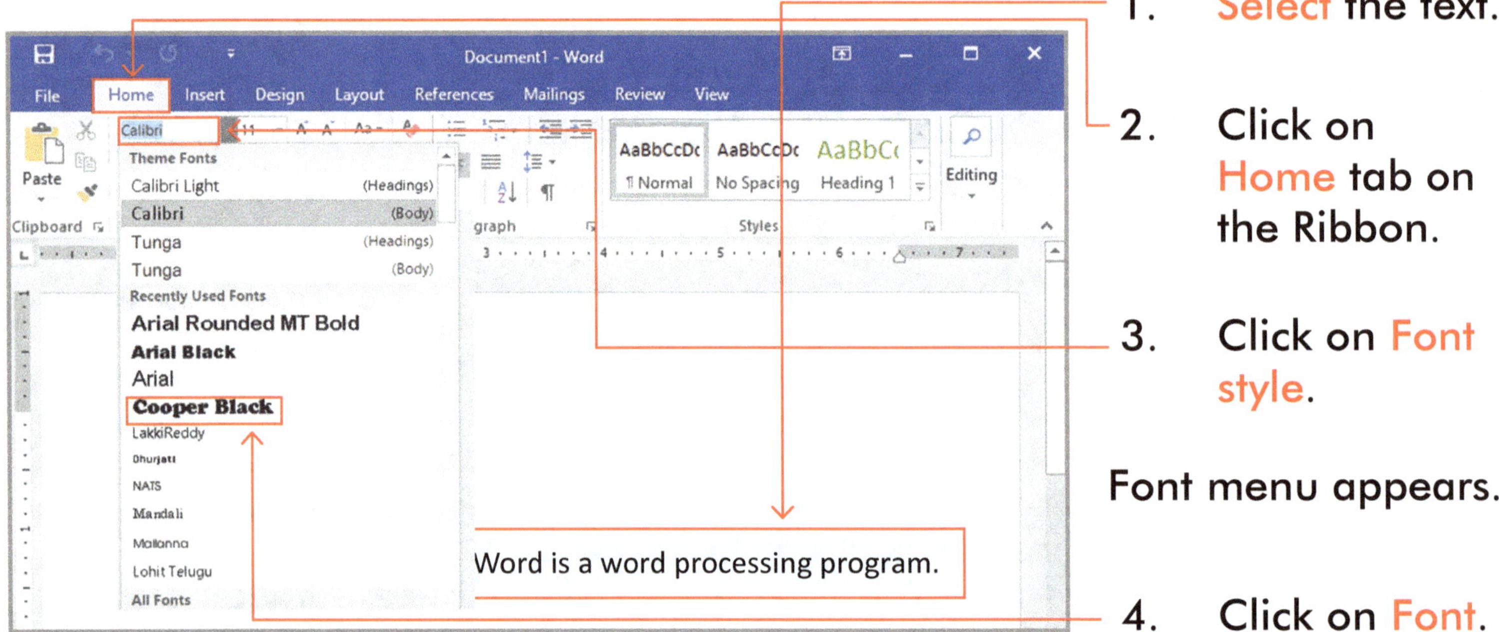


1. **Select** the text.

2. Click on **Home** tab on the Ribbon.

3. Click on **Font style**.

Font menu appears.

4. Click on **Font**.

The text changes in **new font**.

To **deselect** the text, click outside the selected area.

# CHANGE FONT SIZE

This option allows an increase or a decrease in the size of text by choosing different font sizes.

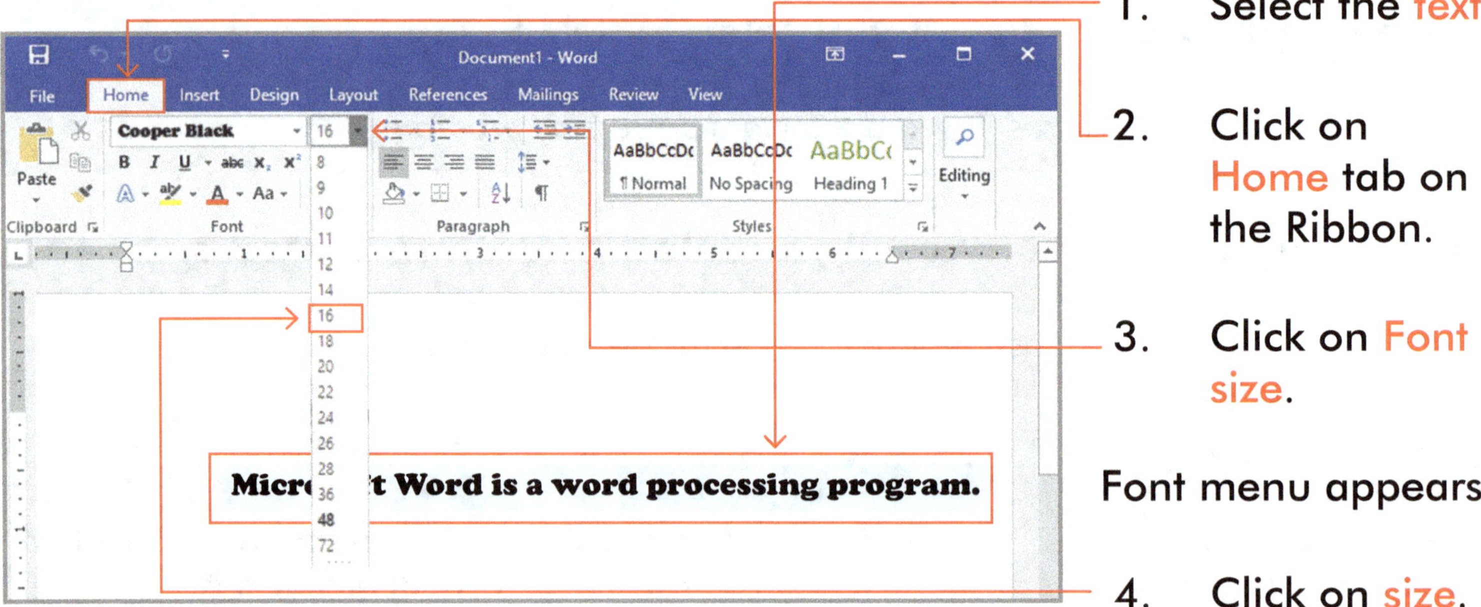


1. Select the **text**.

2. Click on **Home** tab on the Ribbon.

3. Click on **Font size**.

Font menu appears.

4. Click on **size**.

The text changes in **new size**.

To **deselect** the text, click outside the selected area.

# CHANGE FONT COLOUR

You can change the different colours to your text from this option.

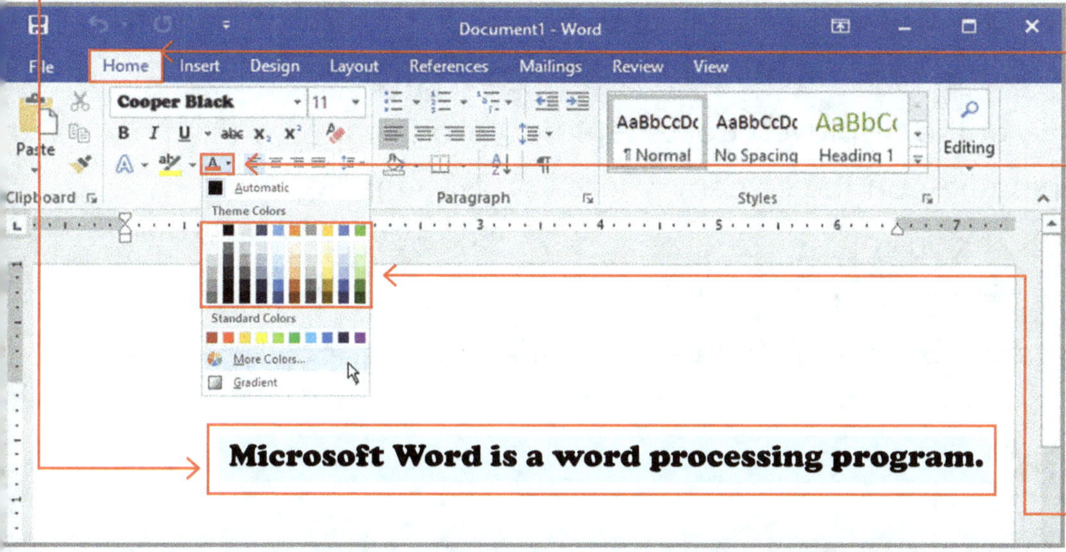

1.  Select the text.

2.  Click on Home tab on the Ribbon.

3.  Click on Font colour.

4.  Click on any colour.

The text appears in a new colour.

To deselect the text, click outside the selected area.

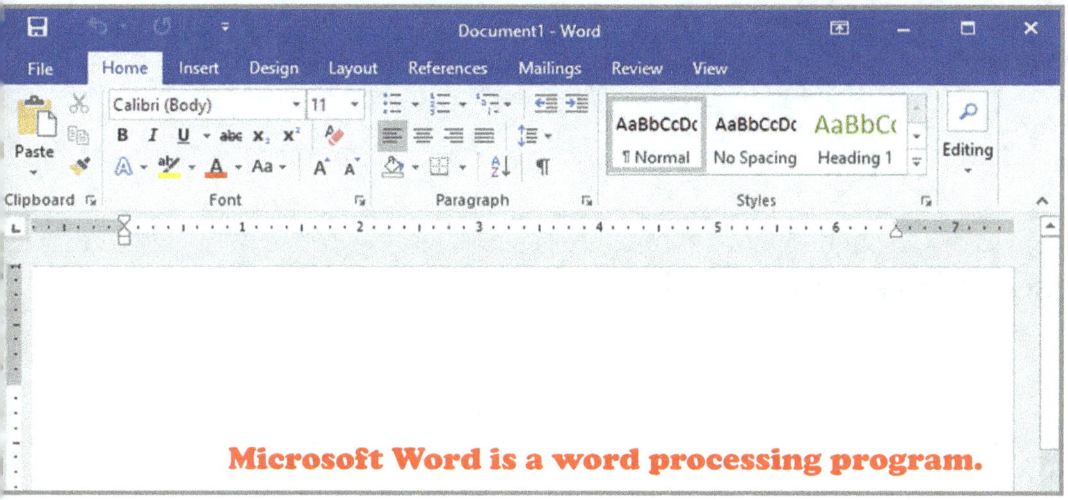

# EXITING FROM THE MS-WORD

After the work is finished, you can exit from Word.

1.  Click on File menu button.

    Backstage view will appear.

2.  Click on Exit.

## LET'S HAVE A LOOK

- MS-Word is a word processing program used to create text documents.
- Documents are the files that you create in the computer.
- With the help of the keyboard, text can be entered into the computer.
- Title bar shows the name of the displayed document and program.
- Insertion point is a flashing line on the screen, where you type the text.
- Word files will have .DOC extension.
- To work with text, first you have to select the text.
- Changing font style, font size, font colour, bold, italic, underline, etc. is called formatting.

## BRAIN TEASER

**1.    Answer the following questions:**

a.    What is MS-Word?

b.    What is the use of Insertion point?

c.    What is Ribbon?

d.    Why do we need to save a document?

e.    Which option is used to make text more thick and dark?

f. Which option is used to put underline in the text?

_______________________________________________

_______________________________________________

g. What is the use of selecting text?

_______________________________________________

_______________________________________________

## 2. Fill in the blanks:

a. _______________________ is a program used to create text document.

b. The topmost bar in MS-Word window is _______________________.

c. A vertical flashing line on the screen is called _______________________.

d. _______________________ helps to make our text more beautiful and colourful.

e. _______________________ option makes your text darker and bolder.

f. _______________________ option is used to make text more slanting.

## 3. Multiple Choice Questions
### Tick (✓) the correct answer:

a. You enter the text with the help of

   i. Mouse ☐   ii. Keyboard ☐   iii. Printer ☐

b. A small blinking vertical line on the work area

   i. Character ☐   ii. Insertion point ☐

   iii. Pointer ☐

c. The shortcut key to save a document

   i. Ctrl + D ☐   ii. Ctrl + S ☐   iii. Alt + S ☐

d. The shortcut key to make the text dark and thick

   i. Ctrl + B ☐   ii. Ctrl + I ☐   iii. Alt + U ☐

## 4. Match the following:

| A | | B |
|---|---|---|
| a. | **B** | <u>Microsoft Word</u> |
| b. | *I* | **Microsoft Word** |
| c. | <u>U</u> | Microsoft Word |
| d. | <u>A</u> | *Microsoft Word* |

# LAB ACTIVITY

**1. Open MS-Word and type the following story:**

### "The Thirsty Crow"

Once there was a crow. He was very thirsty. He found a pot with little water in it.

He got an idea. He put pebbles in the pot. The level of the water rose up. He drank the water and flew away.

**Now, perform the following tasks:**

a. Make a heading "The Thirsty Crow."

b. Change the font size of heading into 24.

c. Change the font size of the remaining text into 18.

d. Change the colour of heading into Red.

e. Change the colour of the remaining text into blue.

f. Save the document with your name.

g. Close the MS-Word window.

**2. Each student can write 10 lines about himself/herself in MS-WORD and save the file.**

# 9 Multimedia and Internet

## MULTIMEDIA

Multimedia is utilizing a combination of media and content of different forms. It is made up of two words—Multi and Media. Multi means more than one or many and Media stands for the sources. Therefore, multimedia is a combination of text, audio, images, video and animation. Most multimedia programs are interactive.

The examples of multimedia are : cartoon movies, animated pictures, etc.

Animated Cartoons

## Importance of Multimedia

According to some specialists:

People recall 20% of what they see, 40% of what they see and hear and 70% of what they see, hear and do.

Multimedia consists of various forms of media, *i.e.* text, graphics, audio, video, animations, etc. The person is able to navigate, interact, create and communicate through it. Therefore, it allows to see, hear and do.

## Multimedia System Requirements

If you want to use multimedia, install the multimedia kit in your computer. The computer that has a capability of presenting multimedia application is called Multimedia System.

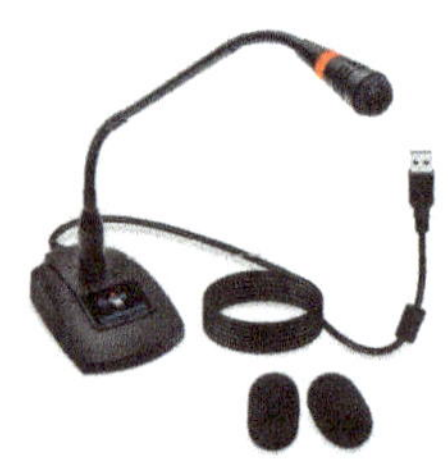

Multimedia Kit

A multimedia system must be having:

1. **CD/DVD drive**: To play CDs and DVDs

2. **Speakers**: To get the sound output

3. **Colour monitor**: To display video and animation

4. **Microphone**: To record the voice

5. **Joystick**: To play games on the computer

## Multimedia Software

There are different types of multimedia software for different types of application areas.

**For example** : Adobe Photoshop for graphics

Adobe Flash for animation

Adobe PageMaker for editing text

Encyclopedia and Atlas for educational purpose.

# Where can Multimedia be used?

Multimedia can be used in various fields for different types of jobs, such as:

⇒ Imparting education

⇒ Listening to songs

⇒ Advertising

⇒ Playing games

⇒ Watching movies and cartoons

⇒ Showing presentations

## Play A Music CD On Computer

You can play an Audio or a Video CD in Windows Media Player (WMP).

WMP is a multimedia software that allows you to listen to songs and watch movies.

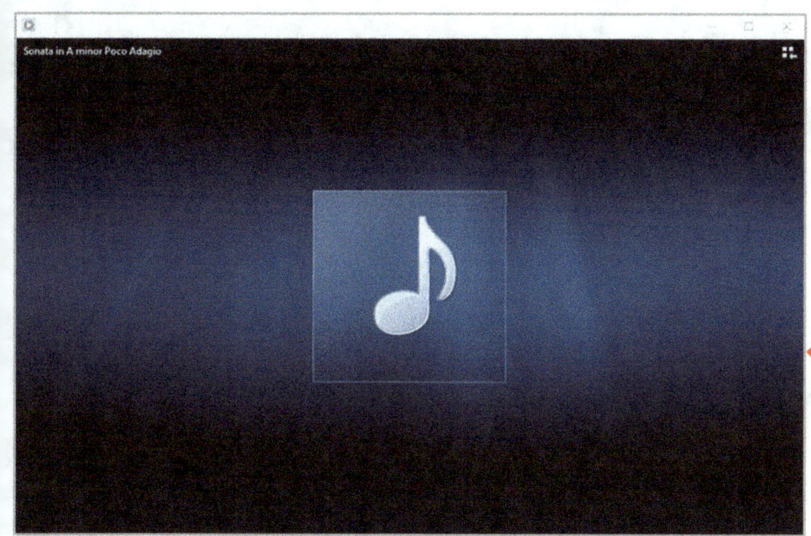


Insert a music CD into the CD or DVD drive of your computer.

The Now Playing window appears and the CD begins playing automatically.

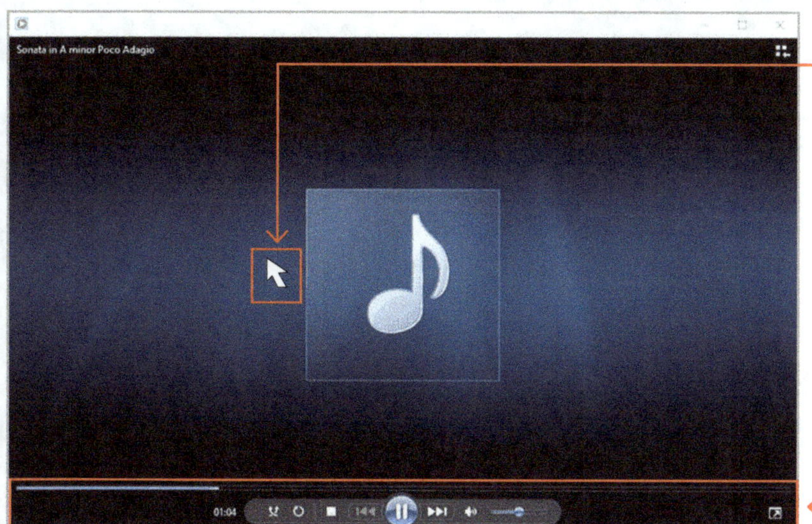


Take the mouse pointer within the Now Playing window.

You can use these controls to stop the CD and then select another song to play or you can pause play if you have to leave the computer.

 # INTERNET

The Internet is a **Global Network** connecting millions of computers. It is a network in which any computer can communicate with any other computer as long as they are both connected via the Internet.

These computers are connected to one another using telephone lines, cables and some wireless media of communication.

With the help of the Internet, one can easily send and receive messages and even talk to others directly sitting in any corner of the world.

Internet

## Components of Internet

The following components are required to get connected to the Internet:

1. A computer
2. A telephone line
3. A modem
4. Internet connection
5. Software

## Uses of Internet

You can use the Internet for many different purposes.

⇒ Searching and sharing Information

⇒ Sending and receiving e-mail messages

⇒ Chatting and making friends

⇒ Buying and selling products

⇒ Listening to music and watching movies

⇒ Playing games

### LET'S HAVE A LOOK

- The word multimedia is comprised of two parts: Multi and Media.

- Multimedia is a combination of content forms: Text, Audio, Still images, Animation and Video.

- The multimedia system must consist of CD/DVD drive, a sound card, speakers, coloured monitors, graphics card, microphone and headphones.
- The Internet is a global network connecting millions of computers.
- The Internet is connected to the computer by means of cables, telephone wires and some wireless media of communication.

## BRAIN TEASER

**1. Answer the following questions:**

a. Define multimedia.

b. What are the requirements of a multimedia system?

c. Where can you use multimedia?

d. Name some of the multimedia softwares.

e. What is the Internet?

f.    What are the uses of the Internet?

g.    Name the components of the Internet.

## 2.    Fill in the blanks:

a.    Multi means ________________ and ________________ mean:
      medium of communication.

b.    Multimedia allows to ________________ , ________________
      and ________________ .

c.    The ________________ connects millions of computers together.

d.    With the Internet, you can easily ________________ and
      ________________ e-mail messages.

## 3.    Multiple Choice Questions
### Tick (✓) the correct answer:

a.    Most multimedia programs are
      i.    interactive ☐        ii.    text-based ☐        iii.    active ☐

b.    It is used to play games
      i.    Joystick ☐           ii.    Microphone ☐        iii.    CD/DVD ☐

c.    Biggest network of computer
      i.    Multimedia ☐         ii.    Monitor ☐           iii.    Internet ☐

d.    The Internet is used for
      i.    Cooking ☐            ii.    Chatting ☐          iii.    Fighting ☐

# Formative Assessment-4
## (Chapters 7-9)

**1. Unscramble the jumbled letters in each group:**

O M C A M S N D

I E I V P T M S R I

U L T E R T

O S M W D R

R T E I N E N T

D I U T E M I L M A

**2. Solve the crossword puzzle:**

a.  LOGO commands

b.  LOGO primitive used to take turtle to the centre of the screen

c.  A combination of media and content of different forms

d.  A group of networks

e.  Small blinking line on screen

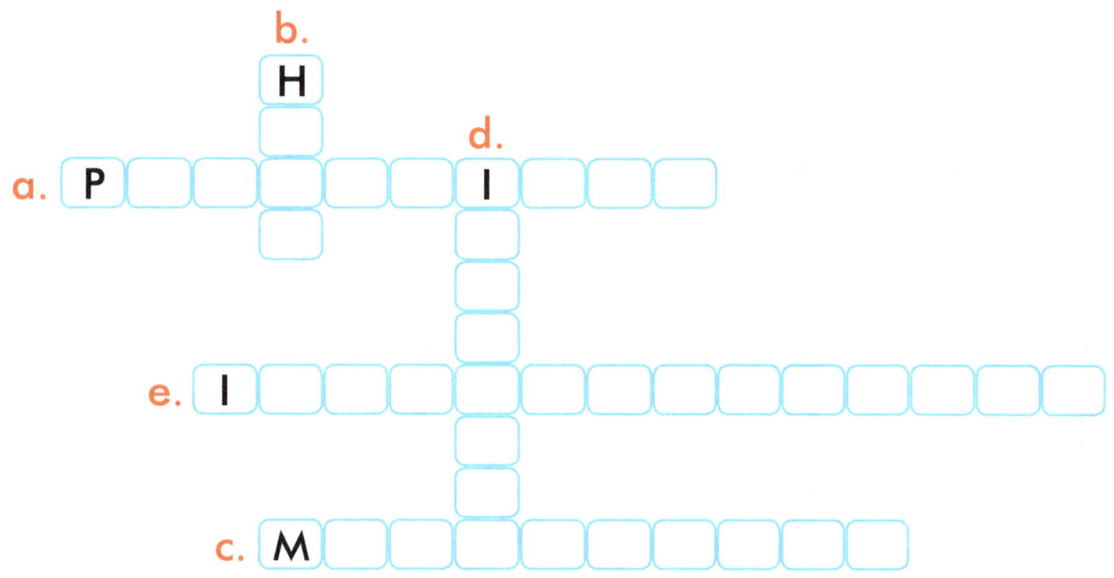

# Summative Assessment-2
## (Chapters 5-9)

**1. Answer the following questions:**

a. What is the use of Flip and Rotate features in Paint?

b. What is LOGO used for?

c. What are primitives in LOGO?

d. What is Turtle?

e. What is Insertion Point?

f. Write the various fields where multimedia can be used.

g. What are the different uses of the Internet?

**2. Fill in the blanks:**

a. LOGO is a ________________ language.

b. ________________ option is used to stretch the image from one side.

c. ________________ feature gives the mirror image of the drawing.

d. ________________ command brings the turtle to the centre of the screen.

e. The Insertion point is ________________ flashing line on the screen.

f. The Internet connects ________________ of computers together.

**3. Write the full forms of the following:**

a. LOGO     b. CD     c. DVD     d. FD

e. HT     f. RT     g. CT     h. CS

i. BK     j. ST

# 10 More About ScratchJr

Coding (a computer program) is giving instructions to the machine (computer) about what action is to be performed.

Computer coding is the use of computer programming languages to give computers and machines a set of instructions on what actions to perform.

ScratchJr is an introductory program (tool) for the young children to create interactive stories, games and animations. Children use it to join the programing blocks together in order to make the character move, jump, dance and sing. Children can modify the character, add their sound and also insert their pictures.

## STEPS OF OPENING ScratchJr

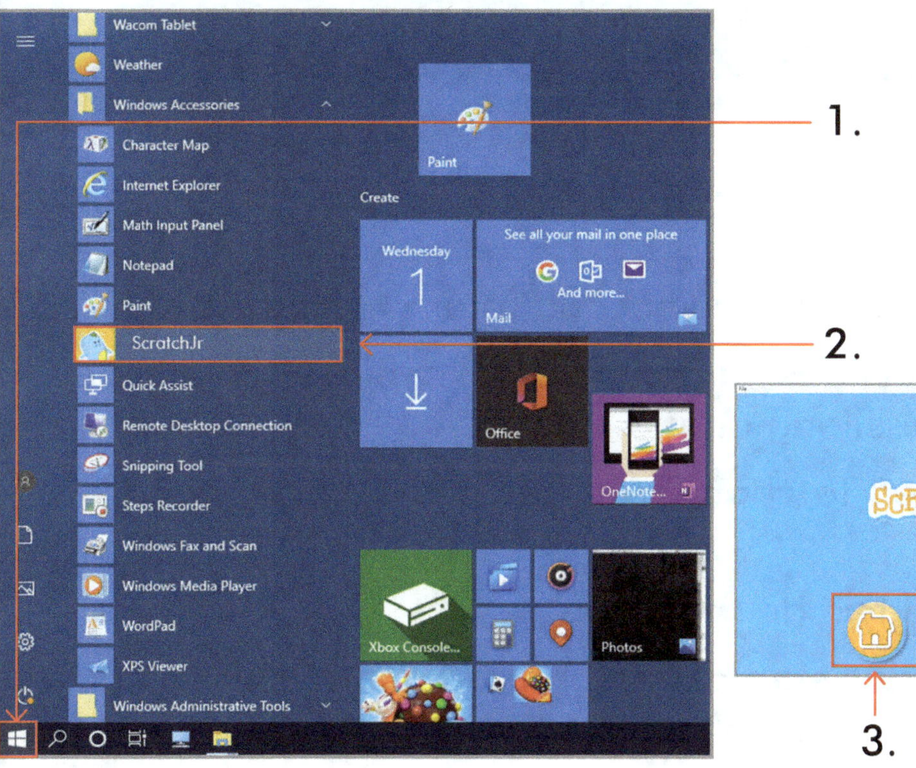

1.  Click Start button.

2.  Select ScratchJr.

3.  Click Home.

4. Click + to open a new project.

## PARTS OF THE SCRATCHJR WINDOW

Let's see and understand the different parts of ScratchJr window.

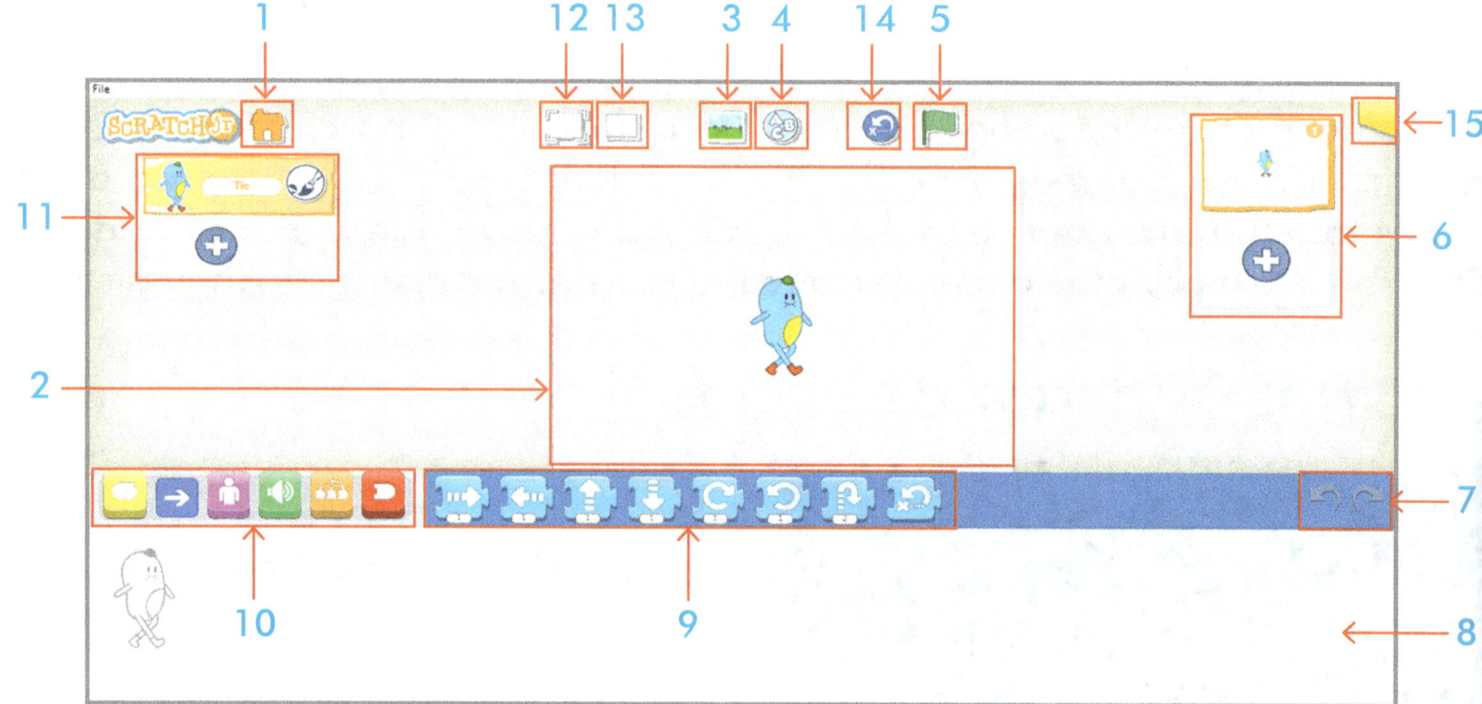


1. **Home button** is used to save the project and return to home page.

2. **Stage** is where all the actions (animation) take place. To delete the character, we need to press long on it.

3. **Background button** is used to change or create the background of the stage.

4. **Text button** is used to add text on the stage.

5. We click on the **Green flag** to start all the programming on the stage that begins with a "Start on Green Flag" block in the script.

6. This button is used to select the different pages in the project. When we click on the plus "+" sign, a new page is added.

7. **Undo or Redo button** is used to undo the mistake in the script.

8. **Programming Area** is the place where you connect the different blocks to make a program.

9. **The Programming Blocks** are used to create a program. You can click and drag the blocks to Programming Area, to make them run.

10. **Block categories** are where you select the category of Programming Block. For example, Blue block is Motion block.

11. **Characters** – Different characters are shown here which are used in the program. Select the character by tapping on it. You can add more characters by clicking in plus '+' sign. And to remove a character, press long on it; a cross sign will appear, click on it.

12. **Presentation button** helps to expand the page to full screen to run the program.

13. **Grid button** is used to toggle the X and Y grids.

14. **Reset button** is used to reset the position of all the characters to their starting position.

15. **Project information**: With this button you can change the title of the project, see all the information about it when it is created and share the project.

## BLOCK CATEGORIES

Let's see the different Block Categories in ScratchJr.

1. Triggering Blocks

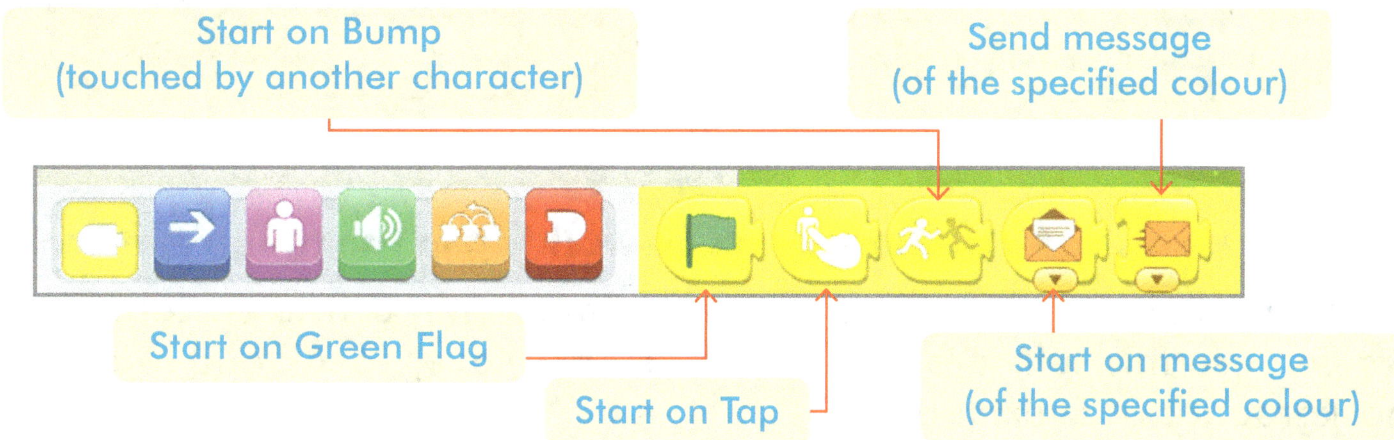

## 2. Motion Blocks

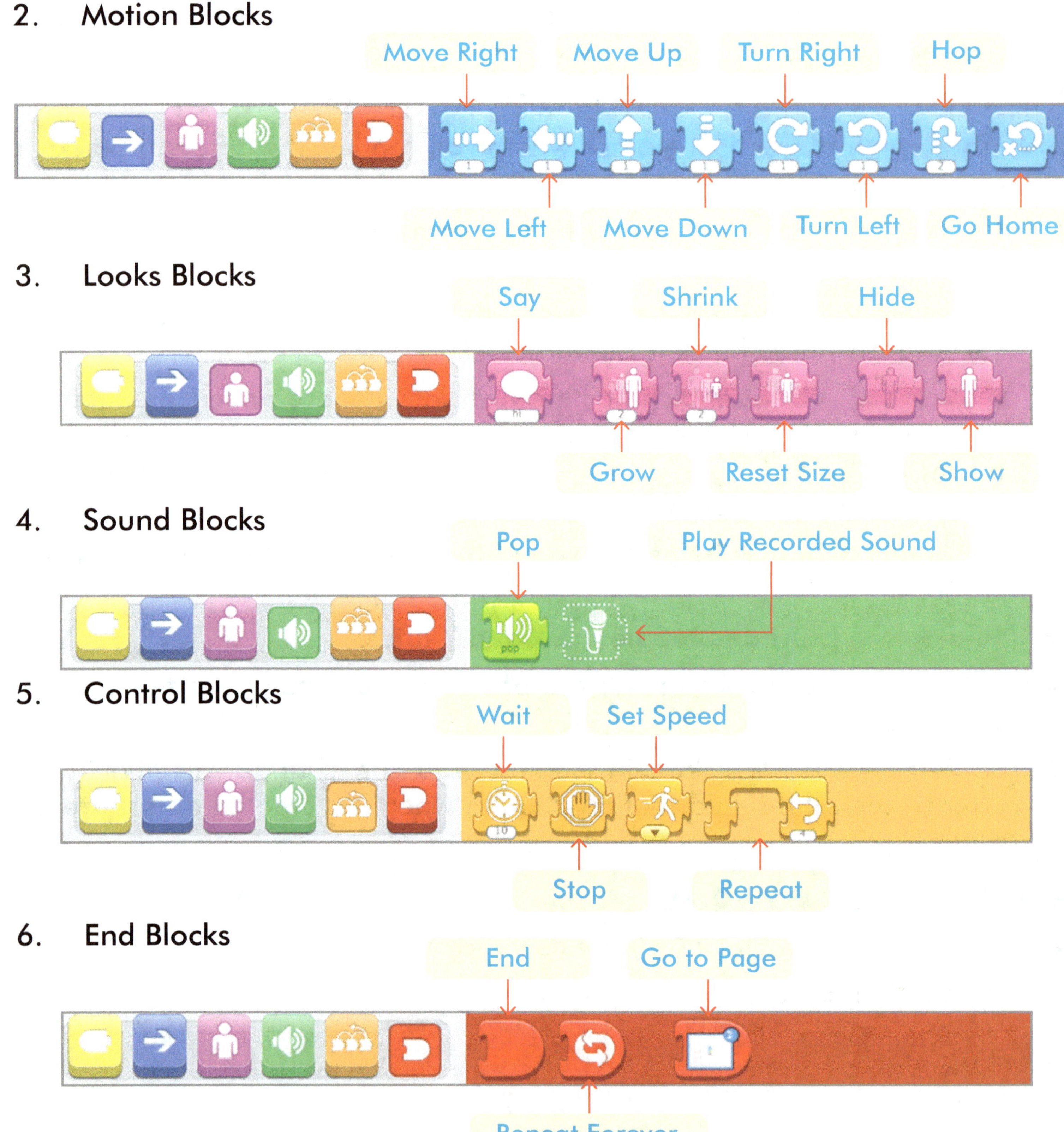


## 3. Looks Blocks

## 4. Sound Blocks

## 5. Control Blocks

## 6. End Blocks

**Let's make a story of mother and son walking to the theatre in ScratchJr:**

In this part, we will learn to make an animation in ScratchJr. Let us see how we can use this software to make our sprite move, speak and to change the backgrounds and text tool.

Open the ScratchJr window.

1. Delete the sprite by a long press on the sprite itself.

2. Click on the **background** button and add a new background **city** to the stage.

We can also draw our own background by using paint icon.

3. Select the desired background and click on ✓ button.

Now, add two new sprites to the stage.

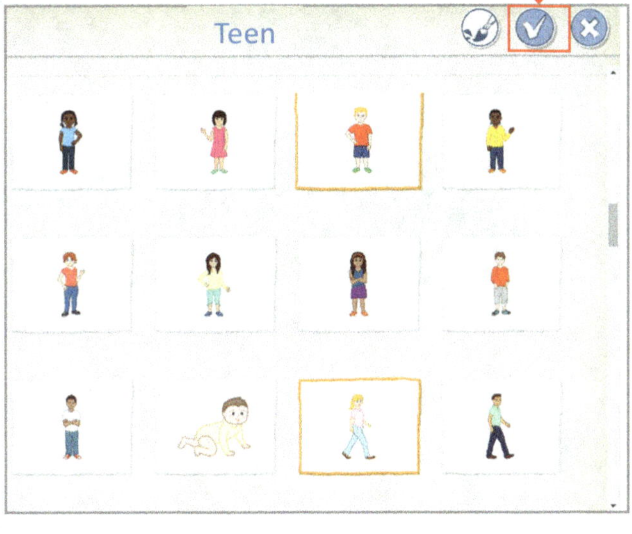

4. Click on the **character** button and add two new characters (one by one- Mother and Child) to the stage.

Now, we will program both the sprites to move and talk to each other. We will use different blocks to program the sprite so that both of them may talk to each other.

5. **Click on the first Character (Mother) button and program the sprite.**

   i.   Click on the Event category and add  (Green Flag) block.

   ii.  Click on the Motion category and add (Move) block. Change the number to 5 (steps).

   iii. Click on Control category and add (Wait) block. Change the number of seconds to 5.

   iv.  Click on Looks category and add (Say) block. Type the message (Wait) on the block.

   v.   Click on Control category and add (Wait) block. Change the number of seconds to 10.

   vi.  Click on Looks category and add (Say) block. Type the message ('Let us go to school') on the block.

6. Click on second Character button.

7. Program the sprite as shown in the figure.

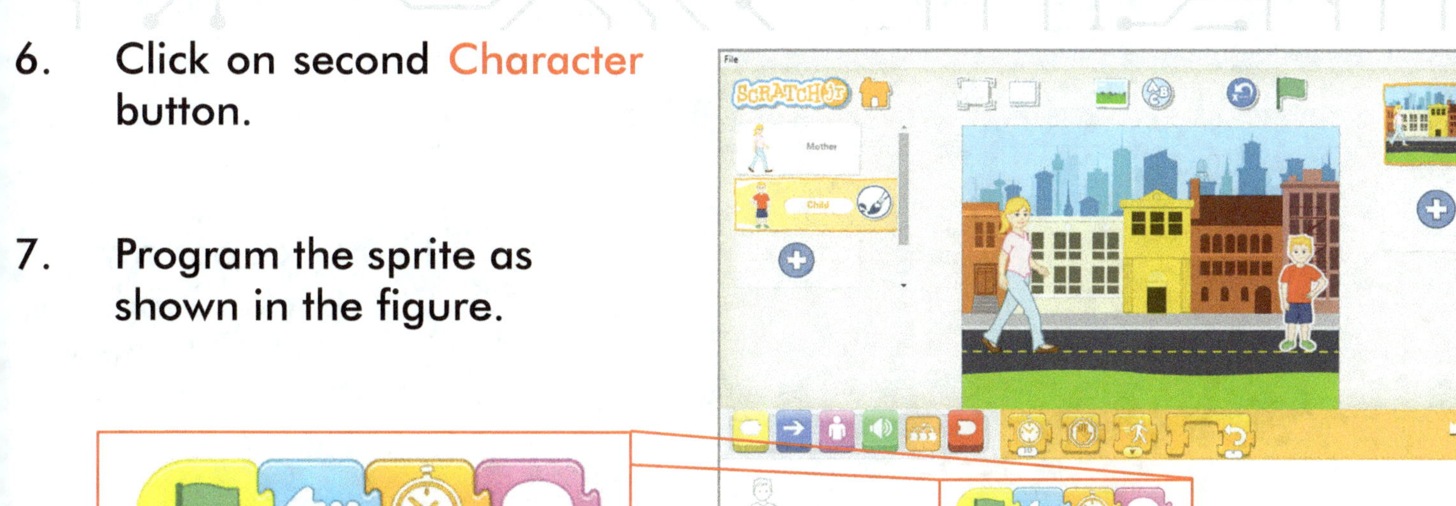

In ScratchJr, we can change the scene to make our story animation more lively and creative. To add a new scene, click on the add page button.

8. Click on the + (plus) sign to add a new page.

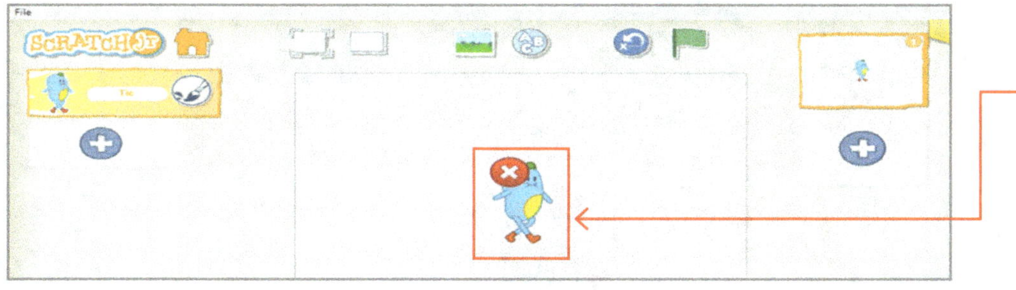

9. Remove the sprite present on the stage by a long press on it.

Add the background to the stage.

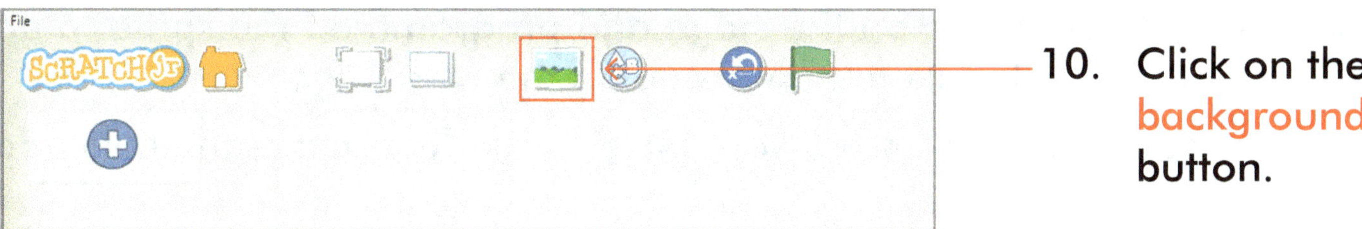

10. Click on the background button.

11. Click on 'city' background and click ✓ button.

The selected background is added to the stage.

To change the scene, we have to program the sprite.

12. Click on the End category and add 🔲 to change the scene.

Try the Script by clicking on the Green Flag.

As we have added new scene on the stage and programmed the sprite to go on the next page, we will make a new scene on the next page.

Add the same Mother and Son who were there in the first scene and also add a fairy.

Now, we will program all the sprites separately to animate the scene.

## Let us program all the sprites in ScratchJr.

⇒ We will program the first mother sprite.

13. Select the first sprite.

Add Green flag block, Move 'block (5) and block from the looks category.

We will program the Child or Son sprite as the same as the Mother Sprite.

14. Select the second sprite.

Code in the same way as shown here.

**Note**

*We can make sprite appear and disappear from the stage by different blocks available in Looks category.*

Now, we will add another scene of a classroom to the stage.

15.   Click on the + (Plus) sign on page section and add Classroom background

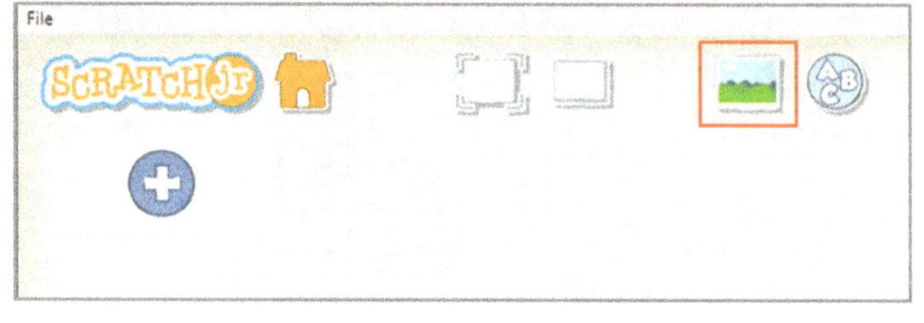

16.   Click on classroom
      background and
      click ✔ button.

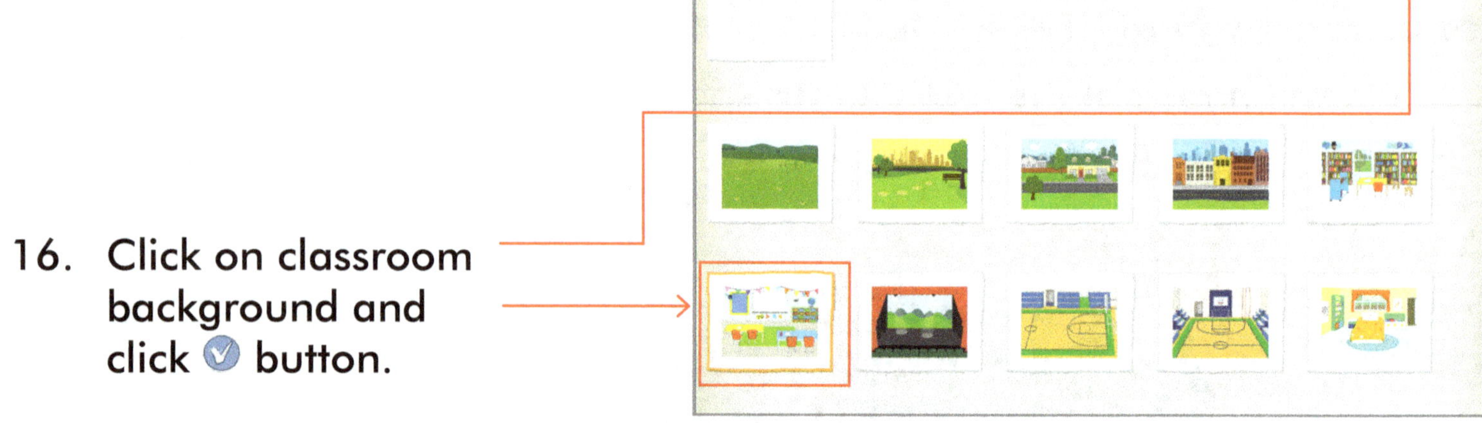

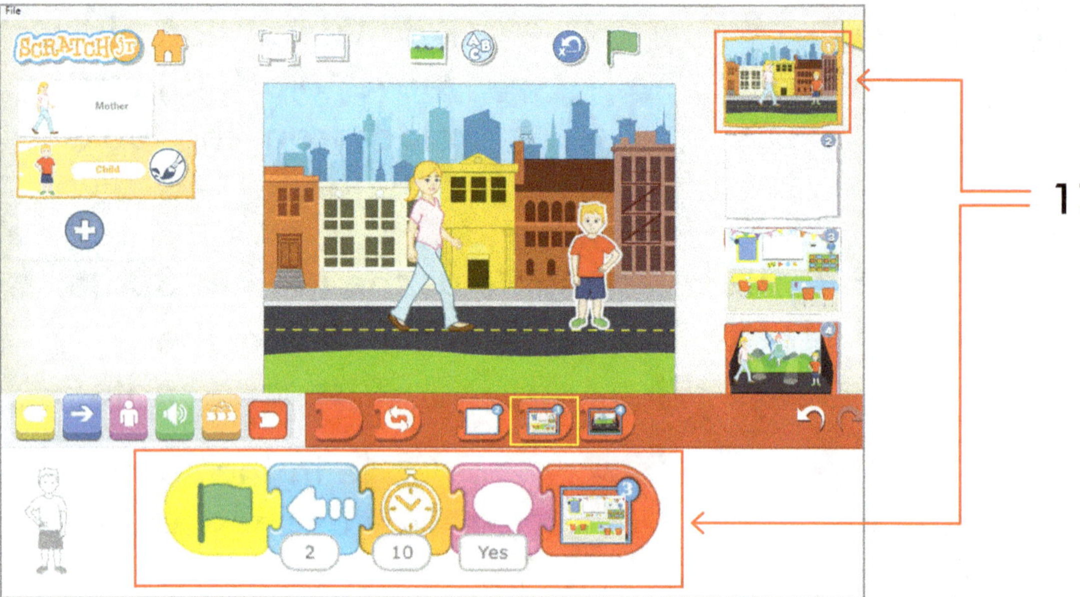

17.   On Scene 2, click
      on End category
      as done on the
      previous page
      and add Scene 3
      block on the fairy
      programming.

Now, try to run the programming script by clicking on the Green Flag.

We will add two girls sprite and a boy sprite on scene 3. Now, we will program
all these three sprites.

We can add text on the stage by clicking on the Text button.

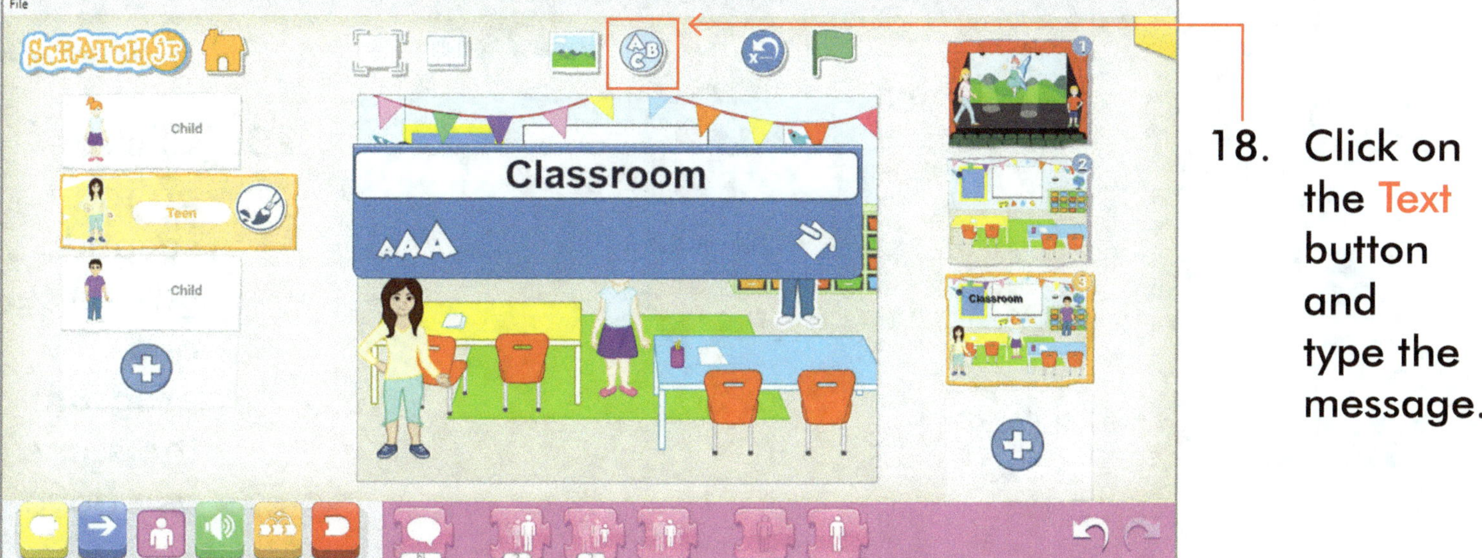

18.  Click on the Text button and type the message.



> **Note**
>
> *We can change the colour and size of the text message.*

We will add Start on Tap block from the Triggering block category. It starts the programming of sprite when you tap on it.

19.  Click on the first girl sprite.

Add block from the Event category, add say block from looks and type the message. Add wait block as well.

20. Click on the second girl sprite and program the same as above.

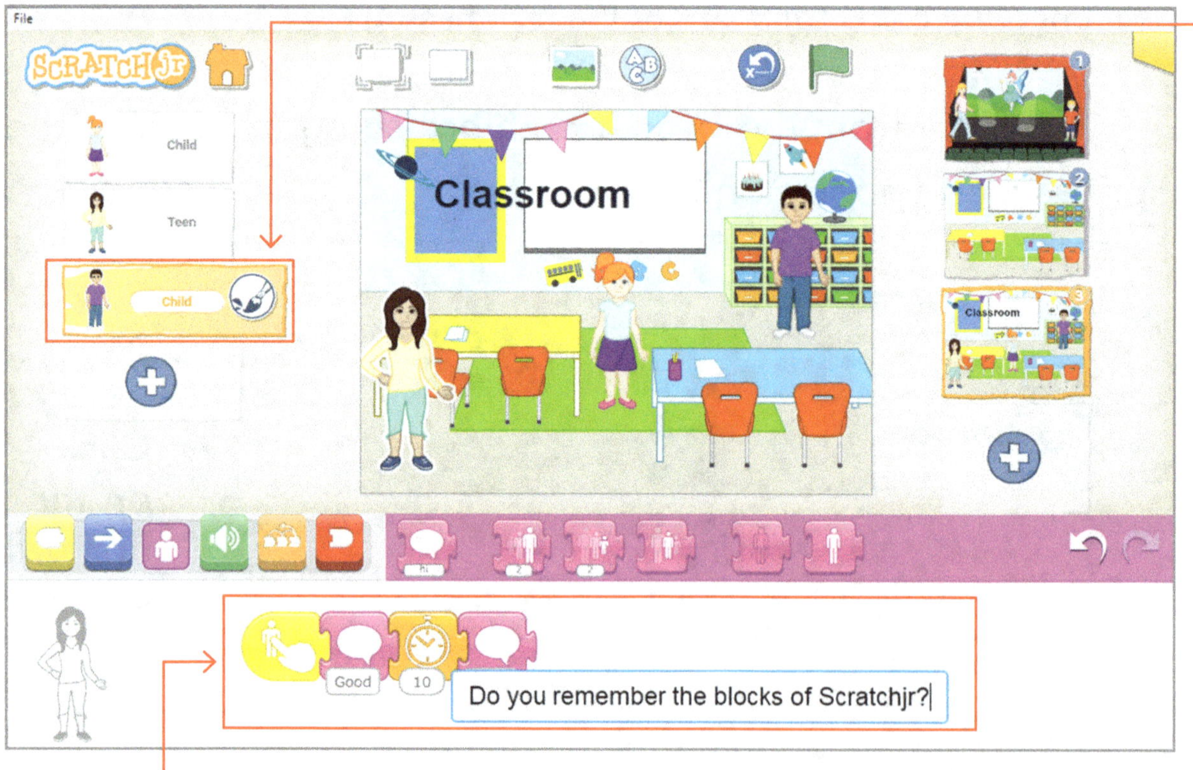


21. Click on the boy sprite.

22.  i.   Add Start on Tap block from the Triggering category.

    ii.   Add Say block from Looks and type the message 'Good Morning'.

   iii.   Add wait block from Control category as well.

    iv.   Add Say block from Looks and type the message.

We have finished our programming part.

Now, we can run this animation by clicking on the Presentation button and then on the Green flag.

## LET'S HAVE A LOOK

- Coding is a special language required by a computer to perform.
- We can make our own stories in ScratchJr.
- The most important thing while making a program in ScratchJr is to drag and connect the different blocks to the Programming Area.
- Presentation button helps to expand full screen to run the program.
- We can make a character appear and disappear from the stage by different blocks available in looks category.

## BRAIN TEASER

**1. Answer the following questions:**

a. What do you mean by coding?


b. Define ScratchJr.

## 2. Multiple Choice Questions

### Tick (✓) the correct answer:

a. What does [image] mean in Looks Blocks?

    i. Shrink ☐     ii. Hide ☐     iii. Say ☐

b. Which of these doesn't belong to Control blocks?

    i. [image] ☐     ii. [image] ☐     iii. [image] ☐

c. Which button runs the program in full screen?

    i. [image] ☐     ii. [image] ☐     iii. [image] ☐

d. What is the colour of the flag that helps to start the program?

    i. Yellow ☐     ii. Green ☐     iii. Black ☐

e. Which of these is the Repeat Forever block?

    i. [image] ☐     ii. [image] ☐     iii. [image] ☐

## 3. Write the functions of the given buttons in ScratchJr.

a. ___________________________________________

b. ___________________________________________

c. ___________________________________________

d. ___________________________________________

e. ___________________________________________

**4.** **What is the use of the following blocks in ScratchJr?**

a.    Hide block

b.    Pop block

c.    Green flag

d.    Wait

e.    Go to page

**5.** **Write the first four steps followed in the ScratchJr.**

## LAB ACTIVITY

**Develop a jungle scene with many trees. Place a zebra, a giraffe, an elephant and monkey on the scene. Program different sprites so that when they are clicked, they may perform different activities.**

- Add different moving blocks to different animals.

- Add text on the screen and give instructions.

- Reduce the sizes of the animals to fit them on the Presentation screen.

- Make each animal do a different activity on tapping.

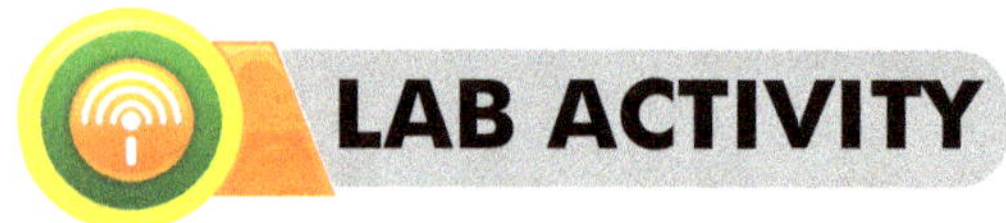